Godly Women

Godly Women

Fundamentalism and Female Power

BRENDA E. BRASHER

COLLEGE OF RIPON
AND YORK ST JOHN
LIBRARY

Rutgers University Press
New Brunswick, New Jersey, and London

Library of Congress Cataloging-in-Publication Data

Brasher, Brenda E., 1952–
    Godly women : fundamentalism and female power / Brenda E.
Brasher.
      p. cm.
    Includes bibliographical references and index.
    ISBN 0-8135-2467-9 (alk. paper).—ISBN 0-8135-2468-7 (pbk. :
alk. paper)
    1. Women in Christianity—United States—Case studies.
2. Fundamentalism—United States—Case studies. I. Title.
BV639.W7B68 1998
277.3'0829'082—dc21   97-17790
                                               CIP

British Cataloging-in-Publication data for this book is available from the British Library

Manufactured in the United States of America

For Stephen . . .

CONTENTS

TABLES

ACKNOWLEDGMENTS

First and foremost, I thank the many Christian fundamentalist women who agreed to be interviewed for this project. Without their willingness to speak with me at length and quite openly about their beliefs and experiences, this book would not have been possible. Though it has been more than a decade since she walked on the earth, I also thank Hannah Ellen, my tall, thin, beautiful, red-haired paternal grandmother. My living memories of her loving heart and fervent religiosity provided a solid, foundational fuel that inspired me through the years of work required to research and write on this topic.

The generosity of colleagues engaged in the academic study of religion is such that I am unable to thank by name all those who listened to my research stories and often gave me very useful feedback on my developing analysis. I do extend a special thanks to those who read and commented upon portions or all of this manuscript during its production, including Donald E. Miller, Stephen D. O'Leary, Robert S. Ellwood, Jon Miller, Nancy T. Ammerman, Virginia Brereton, and D. Paul Johnson.

I owe a particular debt of gratitude to the Women's Caucus of the AAR/SBL, Western Region, for expressing interest in my work at a very early stage. The members of that caucus, including Sheila Briggs, Marilyn Gottschall, Ann Taves, Kathy

Brazeale, Martha Baily, and several others, functioned as a wonderfully critical public forum that helped me think through key portions of my analysis. And, of course, my thanks go to Martha Heller, my Rutgers editor, for her astute advice on how one goes about translating academic prose into a (hopefully) readable book. Finally, I thank the Louisville Institute for their financial support during the writing stages of this book.

Godly Women

Introduction

It was a hazy morning in September. I recently had embarked upon a study of Christian fundamentalist women in the United States, and sat on this day with approximately three hundred women attending the female worship service that regularly closed the Mount Olive weekly women's Bible study. The woman addressing the group was Elaine, the female leader of Mount Olive women's ministries. Giving an impassioned sermon that wrapped up the day's activities, Elaine sweated as she spoke with incredible intensity. The thread of logic connecting the various points she made in her talk was not readily discernable to me; but, the tangible, vivid imagery of her phrases rolled out like a warm, wet cloud that appeared to pull most of the women around me into a cosmos of religious significance. Her words provided a rough, insider's glimpse at some of the hottest issues fueling late twentieth-century fundamentalist political activism in the United States:

> Keep that which is not from you away from your family. Satan knows how to get to us. He goes for the flesh. Think of it. Abortion. He loves blood. Our bone and our flesh. Ourselves and our kids. This year more than other years, we're sensing the shift. When President Clinton can vote for experimental

procedures on an eight-month-old fetus—that's a life—pull out the body and leave the head—to do research for Parkinson's, we're in trouble. Our homes are only as strong as our husbands. Satan doesn't want our husbands strong. He wants our husbands to submit to us, and this will destroy the home. You've got to confront sin. You've got to go up and say, "You're living in sin." Invite them to church. Give them a Bible. Read it to them. Offer to pray with them. Yeah. They'll throw it back in your face. Just say, "You're right. I'm a hypocrite, and a sinner too. So let's pray together. I'll pray for you, and you pray for me." We can change our families by prayer.

The women sitting around me nodded their heads as Elaine spoke, giving bodily signs of assent to her message. Later I learned that most were quite familiar with a startling array of the intimate details of Elaine's life, and almost without thinking *contextualized* her message, heard it against the poignant backdrop those details supplied. For instance, to many the sheer fact that Elaine addressed them at all that day was a sacred miracle. An agoraphobia sufferer for years, Elaine had successfully struggled against a fear that trapped her inside her home and in her struggle was aided by the support and persuasiveness of the fundamentalist women who wanted her to lead them.

An academically trained ethnographer of religion, I mused for some time over how to interpret Elaine's message, along with the other religious events I witnessed that day. During the next few months, as my involvement in fundamentalist congregational women's ministries deepened, I began to accumulate sufficient material and experience to undertake the interpretive challenge that confronted me. But initially, the task seemed one of quasi-Herculean proportions. Although there is general acknowledgment in the historic and sociological literature tracking religious fundamentalism that women have participated in this modern, highly controversial religious phenomenon through-out its brief history, most conventional studies ignore the religious acts of women such as Elaine and those who gathered to hear her. At best, fundamentalist women like Elaine and her female audience are depicted as essentially dedicated to furthering the goals and ideas of fundamentalist men, and thus of ancillary importance to the fundamentalist movement as a whole.

I realized that morning how easy it would be to follow this traditional interpretive path. If I separated Elaine's comments from their context—her condemnation of abortion, her over-arching concern to support a husband's strength—her speech could be deemed evidence supporting a conventional interpretation. But, for me, this context and its significant gender implications were not dismissable. Elaine spoke that morning to an audience of 300 at a time when the average religious congregation in the United States stood at around 120. Women led every aspect of the service that day, from music to Bible teaching, from public worship to the main message, at a time when most of the world's major religious traditions refuse to allow women to lead religious rituals. Overall, Elaine's message encouraged women toward an active engagement of their family life and the world beyond it, telling them that they could shape their husbands actions and alter disruptive familial behaviors at a time when male abdication of familial responsibilities was turning women and their dependent children into the largest percentage of the American poor. And simply by standing up in front of a large group and speaking, Elaine, as the medium of a message, communicated to those present that women, even those who suffered from serious psychological impairments, could become important functionaries in a religious group. The apparent paradox—that fundamentalist women could be powerful people in a religious cosmos generally conceded to be organized around their disempowerment—was intriguing. This book is the result of my effort to discover the extent to which this paradox actually exists in Christian fundamentalist congregations and to analyze the constitutive tensions between content and context that saturate the religious world of Christian fundamentalist women.

Inspired by a desire to understand why Elaine and other women like her join and become actively involved with Christian fundamentalist congregations in the late twentieth century, I became an active participant in two such congregations and for six months attended every women's ministry event they sponsored. The primary data for the book derives from the case studies I developed of these congregations (Elaine's, referred to throughout the text as Mount Olive, and Bay Chapel, also fundamentalist but with a different denominational background) and the women's ministry programs each sponsored. Overall, the book draws upon the observations I made during my field studies, the semistructured interviews I conducted with a variety of Christian fundamentalist women, and the conclusions I eventually reached regarding the import of fundamentalist women's highly gendered religious activities—both to the women themselves, and to the Christian fundamentalist movement as a whole.

While each chapter has its own peculiar nuance, the overarching theme and primary thesis of the book is that to Christian fundamentalist women, the restrictive religious identity they embrace improves their ability to direct the course of their lives and empowers them in their relationships with others. To foster readers' ability to follow me on my adventurous journey into Christian fundamentalism and on what ultimately became a study of the power of fundamentalist women, I open the book with an explanation of the critical importance gender has in fundamentalist congregational life. In addition to the narrow set of religious beliefs that make up the sacred canopy covering each fundamentalist congregation, gender functions as a sacred partition that literally bifurcates the congregation in two, establishing parallel religious worlds: a general symbolic world led by men that encompasses overall congregational life and a second, female symbolic world composed of and led solely by women. In an effort to understand how and why women get involved with these highly gendered religious worlds, I examine an array of fundamentalist women's conversion narratives. Here a critical comparative analysis reveals that cultural gender quarrels that are disempowering women, notably around family issues, are an important motivating factor that influences women's involvement.

The heart of the book details how those women who stay involved with a fundamentalist congregation construct and exercise power within their religious group. As readers will discover, congregational women's ministry programs play an important role in this empowerment. Within the congregation, their women-only activities and events create and sustain a special symbolic world, parallel to the general one but empowering to fundamentalist women. These programs encourage the development of female enclaves, intimate social networks of women that also empower women by functioning as a material and spiritual resource for female fundamentalists in distress and providing a base for political coalition when women wish to alter the patterns of congregational life.

Events that occurred during my fieldwork vividly illustrate the impressive amount of power that fundamentalist women can wield in their communities. Longing for intense, convincing encounters with the transcendent, fundamentalist women become religiously adept through leading and participating in women's ministry programs that cultivate their spiritual abilities. Again an analysis of fundamentalist women's ideas and experiences of faith reveals that the religiosity they develop is a source of considerable power for them.

Most conventional scholarship agrees that fundamentalism

and gender importantly intersect in the area of family life; so, through excerpts from extended interviews with fundamentalist women, I examine whether and how their religious involvement, either in congregational life or in women's ministries, influences their actions within or their attitudes toward their families. Here, I encountered one of the many surprises of this study. Though fundamentalist women insistently claimed that the proper relationship between a woman and her husband is one of submission, they consistently declare that this submission is done out of obedience to God not men and is supposed to be mutual, a relational norm observed by both spouses rather than the capitulation of one to the other. Again, women's interviews divulge how submission increases rather than decreases a woman's power within the marital relationship. In my concluding analysis, I take up the issue of women's involvement with Christian fundamentalism in the United States against the backdrop of contemporary cultural issues and choices and consider the real struggles for power that confront many women and the real choices against which their decisions for or against Christian fundamentalist commitment and involvement are made.

A cardinal goal of any religious ethnography, including this one, is to advance our understanding of lived religion, that is, religion as it is commonly practiced; however, the epistemological ambiguities entailed in ethnographic work are considerable. While gathering the data for this book, I received evangelical pitches intended to convert me and listened for hours to moral assertions obviously intended to travel through me and reach others. Rather than rejecting such overtures, I treated them as an enriching contribution to my research. Image management is not merely a concern of presidents these days. The fundamentalist women I studied are interested in and concerned with their public image, and the level of concern they have about how they are perceived by others is an important aspect of who they are.

When my fieldwork was nearly done, I held a focus group meeting with some of the fundamentalist women I interviewed for the book. During the wide-ranging discussion that took place at that gathering, Mary (Elaine's key assistant and a women's leader in her own right) indicated that when I began the study, she *had* been concerned with her image—with how what she might say and do would be interpreted by me and, through me, by others. But, ultimately, she decided to let go of that concern and trust in her God. To Mary, the bottom line was that if the God she knew and experienced every day did not approve of my research, it would not get done.

As I listened to Mary speak about her faith in relationship to this study, my response to her expression of trust in divine providence was neither one of cynicism nor one of belief. Though I imaginatively toyed with the possibility that a living, active deity oversaw my work, my faith took other forms. But Mary and the other fundamentalist women I met not only trusted the God to whom they prayed, they assumed that God would look after them, even amid an academic research project. Consequently, they spoke openly about their lives and employed what they regarded as the most powerful means they possessed to ensure the best possible outcome of my endeavor. They *prayed* for me and for my work, before and after each interview and during many of the studies and retreats I attended. I always thanked them for these prayers, and must admit I was stirred by them as well. They kept me in touch with the fact that I moved among a people who considered it a reasonable thing to call upon their God to support and guide academic research. As to whether the women were right in their beliefs, well, all who encounter this ethnography must read on and decide for themselves.

Inside a Christian ❋ CHAPTER 1
Fundamentalist
Congregation
A Sacred Canopy
with a Sacred Partition

T his is a book about godly women: the generally well-educated, young to middle-aged, ethnically diverse, Bible-believing women who are integral to the development and survival of Christian fundamentalist congregations across the United States.[1] Rather than offer a general overview of Christian fundamentalist women, it takes up the intriguing challenge of presenting a portrait of Christian fundamentalist women in the particular. It is an exercise, therefore, in microanalysis. What follows is an examination of the life history and spirituality of the women of two Christian fundamentalist congregations in southern California, Bay Chapel and Mount Olive. It is an exploration of how the women who belong to these two congregations function as public actors within them. In the process, it relates how women can and do exercise considerable power in a fundamentalist congregation, and also draw upon the reli-

gious goods they create and discover there to empower themselves at the personal level as well.

In this story, disheveled gender expectations, fragmented
marriages, economic instability, and widespread cultural malaise figure prominently, for fundamentalist women describe
these societal factors as the cultural fuel that propelled them
on a spiritual search . . . one that has led them to the ideas and
activities, friendships, and challenges of a Christian fundamentalist congregation. But to fundamentalist women, the troubles
that moved them toward fundamentalism are important only
to the extent that they led them to become what each now
claims to be: Bible believers who try to live each day in light
of a tangible awareness that a living God exists and watches
over them. Figuring out how one lives this way and what the
boundaries are in such a life is a key topic in women's Bible
study groups, as this excerpt from a discussion among Ann,
Diane, Kiersten, and Carol at a Bay Chapel women's Bible study
illustrates.

> Diane opened the discussion by asking whether it was a sin
> to be angry with God. Kiersten answered, "No, It's not a sin if
> in anger you turn towards God. But it would be a sin if be-
> cause of anger or fear you turn away from God, or if anger
> rules you." Ann added, "Anger, when it becomes bitter, when
> it is eating away at you, is a sin." Carol asked if there was a
> place where believers could draw the line with others. Ann told
> her, "As Christians, we don't have to take it all. We have to
> forgive, but we can take action. We are to act prayerfully, out-
> side of anger. That is our goal. Of course, we're not there yet."

But for many fundamentalist women, trying to get there is the
basic task of life.

Mount Olive and Bay Chapel

Today across the United States, millions of people identify themselves as Bible-believing, fundamentalist Christians. Among the manifold congregations that these people join, the two I studied in depth are Mount Olive and Bay Chapel. Mount Olive is a congregation of approximately four thousand people situated in a working-class, ethnically diverse urban neighborhood. Bay Chapel is a congregation of roughly two thousand located in a predominantly white, middle-class suburb. Mount Olive is loosely affiliated with Calvary Chapel, a thirty-year-old Christian movement started by Chuck Smith in southern California that now includes more than 550 congregations spread across the United States. Bay Chapel belongs to the Foursquare Gospel denomination started by evangelist Aimee Semple McPherson but is part of the fifty-congregation Hope Chapel reform movement begun by Ralph Moore in the 1970s. Both the new Christian movement initiated by Smith and the reform movement started by Moore include a pronounced effort to focus communal gatherings on a rational approach to an avowedly inerrant Bible; yet each has more than a few tendrils in the American Pentecostal tradition. Sociologists who have studied the home church of the Calvary Chapel movement in Costa Mesa, California, describe its religious ethos as "experiential fundamentalism" (Richardson and Davis 1983, 397) and "California kick back" fundamentalism (Balmer 1992, 12).[2]

At Mount Olive and Bay Chapel, communal expectations favor serious religious commitment and heavy religious involvement. To meet believers' high demands, each congregation offers programming from early morning until far into the evening every day of the week, including multiple worship services on Sunday. Mount Olive maintains an on-site Christian school for youth. Bay Chapel sponsors Sunday services in two buildings several blocks apart, because its main facility is insufficient to house all who wish to attend.

The two congregations are alike in that an essentially identical sacred canopy marks off the religious life of each. The cardinal theological ideas that constitute the threads of this canopy include an inerrant Bible, the virgin birth and bodily resurrection of Jesus, and premillennialism, that is, a belief that the second coming of Jesus (the parousia) will precede the millennium, the thousand-year Kingdom of God (Ammerman, 1987; Balmer, 1992; Barr, 1977). To say that these ideas form a canopy under which members take shelter is not simply a sociological observation. It is a publicly acknowledged truth proclaimed by the pastoral staffs at Mount Olive and Bay Chapel, as this excerpt from a sermon by Mike (Mount Olive's senior pastor and Elaine's husband) makes clear. "The church today as a whole is hurting. The church as a whole is not teaching the word of God, so the people aren't getting fed. They aren't getting the victory. They're having religious services and feeling good when they go there [to church], but they don't have anything to use when they are out in the marketplace. They don't have anything that's changing their hearts and their lives and giving them a philosophy of living. People are coming to this place just like an oasis in the midst of famine in the land."

Yet the sacred canopy that covers congregational life at Mount Olive and Bay Chapel is comprised of more than theological ideas. Certain social maxims constitute part of its fabric as well. Commitments to strong gender differentiation and heterosexual marriage as necessary features of the ideal lifestyle for adults are as fervently upheld by the pastoral leadership as the acceptance of theological concepts such as Jesus' virgin birth. Marking these congregations most obviously as fundamentalist is the attitude that prevails within them of mistrust toward social institutions outside the church. Many Mount Olive and Bay Chapel members home-school their children. At Mount Olive, members also have the option of enrolling their children in the congregation's grade school. In spite of the enormous

personal and financial expenses involved in the private schooling of offspring, most members opt for one of these two choices.
Few enroll their children in public schools. For the members
of these fundamentalist congregations, almost any price seems
worth paying to keep their children out of public schools—
institutions that many fundamentalists perceive to be, as Susan Rose once aptly described it, in "the hands of Satan" (Rose
1988).

Woven together, these notions and attitudes create a sacred
canopy that distinguishes those who attend Mount Olive and
Bay Chapel as true believers, a people set apart. But although
the sacred canopy that extends over congregational life putatively covers all, its sheltered expanse is not the same for everyone who steps under it. This is because the sacred canopy
of fundamentalist beliefs and attitudes that supposedly unites
all believers includes a sacred wall of gender that bifurcates
them. Composed of gender-driven rules and patterns, ideas and
architecture, a sacred gender wall exists in these fundamentalist
congregation which separates those who attend into what are
treated as two ontologically distinct groups: women and men.

Like the sacred canopy of theological beliefs and attitudes,
the sacred gender walls at Mount Olive and Bay Chapel are
nearly identical. The primary ingredient of its bricks and mor-
tar is the idea that women and men have been divinely created as different types of beings who, while belonging together
in heterosexual marriage, have dissimilar tasks to accomplish
while on earth. The habits of gender that construct and maintain the sacred wall permeate the social worlds of Mount Olive
and Bay Chapel and in the process guarantee that discrete
means and methods of religious life for women and men are
an integral aspect of congregational involvement.

At Mount Olive and Bay Chapel, men draw upon the presence of the sacred gender wall to claim almost all congregational
authority for themselves; thus, among other things, the wall

guarantees that the senior pastorate at both churches is reserved for males, as are seats on the executive advisory board
of either congregation. Equally significant, though considerably
less reflected upon in academic analysis, women at each congregation utilize the presence of the sacred gender wall to ra-
tionalize the development of extensive ministry programs run
exclusively for, and managed solely by, themselves. Female newcomers to Bay Chapel or Mount Olive rapidly discover that for
them the congregation as a whole is not the sole provider of
religious goods. Alongside the male-dominated symbolic world
of overall congregational life exists a parallel symbolic world
administered totally by women. The plethora of women's ministry programs that supports these female symbolic worlds simultaneously establishes and nurtures female enclaves, separate,
sociocultural networks of women. A cardinal finding of my research is that these enclaves largely function as self-legitimating
female domains and play a cardinal role in the construction of
female power in overall congregational life.

At Mount Olive, one-fifth of all women are actively involved
in the women's ministry programs and thus participate in the
female enclave that the sacred gender partition creates. At Bay
Chapel, one-third of all women are similarly involved. There,
the programs that contribute to the formation of the enclave
include five women's Bible studies, a biannual women's retreat,
a monthly women's outreach luncheon, an ongoing women's
prison outreach ministry, a monthly women's breakfast, and
various other special programs for women. Mount Olive offers
a weekly women's Bible study, an ongoing Sisters-in-Service
program, women's aerobics, an annual women's retreat, a bi-
monthly evening women's ministry program, a sexual abuse vic-
tims group, a women's counseling program, a counseling/
adoption agency that provides support for pregnant women, and
assorted other specialized programming.

At each, the core women's ministry program is the women's

Bible study. At Mount Olive, an average of 210 women attend the weekly women's Bible study, which runs for nine months of the year. At Bay Chapel, 200 women attend one of five different women's Bible study groups that run year round. At both churches, women's spirituality retreats, monthly luncheons, and monthly evening meetings consistently fill to capacity the hall or retreat center in which they are held. At all women's ministry events, women are the speakers, table leaders, musicians, and film/tape crew as well as the attendees.

During the Bible studies, detailed examination of biblical texts takes place in a small study/prayer cell cluster of eight to ten women. These cell groups are the crucial social units that make up the female enclave in a fundamentalist congregation, for involvement in a cell group has significant lifestyle implications for a woman. It embeds her in a network of intimate connections that can and, most often, do play a major role in her life. Each week in her cell cluster, women in intimate connection with other women work out their emotions, acknowledge and pray for each other's psychic wounds, and come to an accord on the meaning of faith. During cell group meetings at Mount Olive and Bay Chapel, women with young infants casually breast-fed their babies, because there was no social censure for publicly nurturing infants and no male present who might view an exposed breast as an erotic object. In one cell group meeting I attended at Mount Olive, fundamentalist women alternately laughed, talked about Jesus, argued about the Bible, and cried over personal misfortunes, and then proceeded to compare how babies were responding to a newly designed high chair. Such a range was deemed acceptable because these groups existed, according to the cell group participants and leaders, precisely for the purpose of feeding and strengthening the faith of women by responding to the concerns of their daily lives. Although cell groups are the basic units in which Bible studies take place, their activities stretch beyond the study per se. Once a group is established, its members may gather for breakfast, get together with their families for picnics, or even begin to celebrate birthdays, anniversaries, and other life passage events as a group. Some cell groups have their members pair up and telephone each other every morning to offer prayer and encouragement for the day. Typically, for each formal meeting a cell group has there is at least one informal social event as well.

Given the frequency and intimacy of these interactions, cell group participants tend to develop great affection for each other. Consequently, the members of a cell group are those to whom a woman often turns to when crises arise. At Bay Chapel one day, a woman began crying the moment she sat down at the table with her group. Between wrenching sobs, she revealed that she had left her physically abusive husband the day before and spent the night in her car. As table-mates comforted her, the table leader invited the distraught woman to move into her home; then, the group began working out the details of the move.

Membership Demographics

The membership profiles of Mount Olive and Bay Chapel are remarkably similar: young adults and young married couples dominate the membership rolls at each. According to congregational surveys conducted for this research project, 62 percent of Mount Olive attendees are in the peak family development years of twenty-six to forty-five years old.[3] At Bay Chapel, 72 percent of attendees are of this generative-prone cohort. Racial characteristics of the membership at each generally reflect the surrounding community. At Mount Olive, 65 percent of the membership is white, 28 percent is Mexican-American, 3 percent is Asian-American, 2 percent is African-American, and 2 percent is other. At Bay Chapel, 84 percent of the membership is white, 8 percent is Mexican-American, 4 percent is Asian-American, 2 percent is African-American, and 2 percent is other.

The life characteristics of the Bay Chapel and Mount Olive women I interviewed differ, but not dramatically enough to raise major questions about whether qualitatively different social dynamics are at work in each. Most of the women were in their thirties (11 of 23 at Bay Chapel; 15 of 24 at Mount Olive). The next most frequent cohort was in the forties for Mount Olive women (6 of 24), but in the twenties for the women of Bay Chapel (5 of 23). Women's educational levels were high for both congregations. All the women I interviewed had graduated from high school. The majority had completed at least some college (11 of 23 at Bay Chapel; 14 of 24 at Mount Olive). At Mount Olive, six were college graduates, with half also having completed master's-degree work. Seven Bay Chapel women were college graduates. Two had completed master's programs as well. These levels of educational attainment are startlingly high when compared to the rest of American Christians. According to Roof and McKinney's study of American mainline religion, Bay Chapel and Mount Olive women are more highly educated than most Catholics, other conservative Protestants, black Protestants, moderate Protestants, and those described as "Others" (Roof and McKinney 1987, 112).[4]

The racial/ethnic characteristics of the women proved quite elusive. Here qualitative analysis, a method whose forte is its sensitivity to the complexities of lived human experience, delivered more than I expected. When I asked women about their racial/ethnic identity in open-ended interviews, the answers they gave were frustratingly messy to categorize. For instance, Andrea, a young, dark-brown–skinned Bay Chapel adherent, described her racial/ethnic heritage as "southern," "Georgian," and "military." This type of eclectic response was not unique to Andrea. My interviewees consistently described their racial/

ethnic characteristics in an almost perverse fusion of cultural, social, and geographic terms.

Maria typifies the response of many. She explained that both her parents were born in Mexico. They came to the United States before she was born and intentionally reared her Anglo, making sure she knew no Spanish and felt no connection to their Mexican cultural heritage. "We didn't celebrate Cinco de Mayo when I was growing up, for instance," she said. Maria considered herself American. For Angela, Maria's five-year-old daughter, things were different. Fascinated by her maternal grandparents' history, Angela was taking Spanish dance classes. Now contentedly ensconced in American life, Maria's parents had relaxed their language rules a bit and spoke to Angela in their native tongue. As a result, Maria's daughter—a second-generation American—was nearly bilingual; thus, it was Angela who possessed the hybrid cultural identity of "Mexican American," which Maria, a first-generation citizen, claimed she herself definitely did not.

Almost all my Mount Olive interviewees were married (23 of 24). The majority of the Bay Chapel interviewees also were married (15 of 23), but a notable number were single (8 of 23). I attribute the presence of a higher number of single women among my interviewees at Bay Chapel to the social fact that Bay Chapel offers special programs for single women, thus drawing them into women's ministries, whereas Mount Olive does not. A high percentage of the women I interviewed were mothers (13 of 23 at Bay Chapel; 19 of 24 at Mount Olive). Slightly more than half had at least one child still living at home (14 of 24 at Mount Olive; 12 of 23 at Bay Chapel).

The women at Bay Chapel were much more significantly involved in wage-earning work outside the home than the women of Mount Olive. Exactly half of the Mount Olive interviewees claimed to be involved in no wage-earning work. This was a marked contrast to the Bay Chapel women, only one-fourth of whom (6 of 23) described themselves as being uninvolved with for-pay work outside the home. Contrarily, more Mount Olive women worked part-time than Bay Chapel women (8 of 24 versus 5 of 23). In terms of work, the largest differential between the two was in full-time employment. Over half of the Bay Chapel women were engaged in full-time wage-earning work, compared to one-sixth of the Mount Olive women (12 of 23 versus 4 of 24). The demographic factor that offers the most likely explanation for at least part of these differences in work involvement is the significantly higher proportion of working-age single women at Bay Chapel (slightly over one-third of Bay Chapel women were single, while only one Mount Olive interviewee was). Though I was not able to operationalize and test the possibility, simple economics may be the second key factor in this disparity. It takes a substantially higher income to live in proximity to Bay Chapel's oceanfront site than it does to reside under the urban umbrella of Mount Olive.

Gender and Christian Fundamentalism

A controversial phenomenon, Christian fundamentalism is described in much academic literature as a spiritually militant, fervently apocalyptic, worrisomely antimodern socioreligious movement. Nonfundamentalists' fears about what such inordinately religious people might do has inspired a wide-ranging scrutiny of Christian fundamentalism—increasingly lumped together with the fervent religious movements of other world religions—and has generated a mini-industry of fundamentalism studies, ranging from the University of Chicago's multivolume *Fundamentalisms Observed* to public media coverage such as the 1996 television news special on the Promise Keepers men's movement. Recently, a critical breakthrough in this research has come from twentieth-century scholars who privilege gender as a category of analysis. These scholars argue that the way this modern religious movement typically has been studied and portrayed elides the primary meaning of gender within it. The inattendance to gender by religionists and by scholars of religion has made it possible for Christian fundamentalism to be defined by its adherents as a religious movement whose central concern is orthodoxy or "right belief" and by scholars as a social movement whose primary impetus is resistance to modernity. Both definitions marginalize the curious parallel timing between the rise of Christian fundamentalism, with its gender-conservative ideology and practices, and the widespread cultural movement toward liberalization of gender patterns.

In a landmark work, *Ungodly Women: Gender and the First Wave of American Fundamentalism*, Betty DeBerg presented the first extended criticism of the usual approaches to fundamentalism. DeBerg insisted that gender was not a minor issue of family norms for Christian fundamentalism but the cardinal factor that triggered the birth of the movement. Through a detailed reading of the sermons and writings of its first generation of male leaders, DeBerg disclosed how the prevailing rhetoric of fundamentalism's first wave was impelled by early twentieth-century antifeminist backlash against the expanding rights of women. Pushing our understanding of gender issues in fundamentalism even further, Margaret Bendroth subsequently undertook an historical appraisal of the role of gender in fundamentalist parachurch organizations. The book she wrote out of that research, *Fundamentalism and Gender*, concisely traced how the gender ideologies of fundamentalist parachurch institutions became more restrictive toward women's leadership in response to cultural antifeminist sentiments.

My research project was formulated to address a serious gap in the developing body of literature on the significance of gender for Christian fundamentalism: the involvement of women in Christian fundamentalist congregations. As in DeBerg's study of fundamentalist rhetoric and Bendroth's study of fundamentalist parachurch organizations, this study privileges gender as a category of analysis. But while DeBerg and Bendroth studied Christian fundamentalism's roots, I study its present; and where DeBerg and Bendroth surveyed the ideas of fundamentalist men and parachurch institutions, I examine fundamentalist congregational life and the voices of women instrumentally involved in its activities. Supporting the conclusions of DeBerg and Bendroth, my research findings affirm the centrality of gender for Christian fundamentalist ideas and practices. At fundamentalist congregations, gender organizes material and ideal religious life—from worship to administration, from social interaction to architecture. My findings also reinforce DeBerg's and Bendroth's observations that what many fundamentalist believers overtly claim to be purely religious ideas and behaviors are significantly informed by cultural gender quarrels.

One of the most critical findings of my study of the intersection of gender and fundamentalist congregational life is that women consistently form all-female groups within fundamentalist congregations that run parallel to mixed-sex congregational activities. These ministries form social networks among women that provide them with a valuable source of religious alterity and institutional power. For when fundamentalist women want to exercise power, want to change their congregation in any way, these groups provide them with an organizational base from which to operate.

Mount Olive, Bay Chapel, and Christian Fundamentalism

Throughout the book, I refer to Mount Olive and Bay Chapel as Christian fundamentalist congregations and the women who attend them as female fundamentalists. Behind these labels lies considerable diversity, as later chapters make clear. Although Christian fundamentalism is treated in much academic literature and by the media as a cohesive movement, it is in fact exactly the opposite. There is substantial disagreement among fundamentalists over who or what qualifies as a fundamentalist; and, while fundamentalists claim to possess clear, uniform ideals, Christian fundamentalist institutions can and do exhibit considerable diversity. Because of this, Mount Olive and Bay Chapel should not be interpreted as typifying fundamentalism as a whole; they are rather two groups contributing to the diverse phenomenon which is late twentieth-century fundamentalism.

Associated with relatively new Christian movements, Mount Olive and Bay Chapel show noticeable traces of their recent inception in the cultural customs that tend to prevail at them. Dress is casual. Services are offered at flexible times and on a variety of days of the week, to accommodate the schedules of those whose lives move to the irregular rhythms of postindustrial work. Music, a crucial component of the groups' cultural appeal, takes its cue from popular youth trends. Musicians adapt stylistic elements from American pop music to compose jazzy choruses of faith. Lively, rhythmic music composes at least a third of every event, during which adherents sing, clap, and at times stomp along to Christian rock, rap, folk, and Latin jazz sounds. At both Bay Chapel and Mount Olive, it is the musical segment of community rituals that is called "worship." The remainder of the service is referred to as Bible study.

Another indicator of these congregations' newness is the profusion of activities they offer that have sympathetic ties to the personal growth movement. From individualistic, public, confessional conversions to self-authoritative Bible studies, the religious goods of Bay Chapel and Mount Olive are directed to appeal to an audience of individuals interested in drawing upon religious experiences to better their own sense of (generally, psychological) well-being. Yet the leaders of Mount Olive and Bay Chapel are attempting to missionize not only rock music but also the therapeutic pattern so dominant in modern life. Similar to the charismatic Catholics Mary Jo Neitz studied, Bay Chapel and Mount Olive leaders embrace activities geared toward the transformation of individuals, with the expectation that those who achieve such transformation will then help facilitate the transformation of others (Neitz 1987).

The normative teachings that dominate at Mount Olive and Bay Chapel have their origin in Evangelical Protestantism, an interpretation of Christianity that takes as its central tenet "a definite, deeply experienced personal relationship with Jesus Christ" (Ellwood 1973, 30). Yet within American Christianity, Bay Chapel and Mount Olive exhibit more affinity with conservative evangelical Protestantism than its more liberal manifestations. Another word for conservative evangelical Protestantism is fundamentalism.

According to Jerry Falwell, fundamentalism is "the religious phenomenon of the twentieth century" (Falwell 1981, 1). Historically at least, Falwell has the date right: the first wave of fundamentalism surfaced in the United States at the turn of the century. As an institutional phenomenon, fundamentalism began as an ecclesial schism within Protestantism. It was a struggle between conservative, predominantly Calvinist Protestants and moderate-to-liberal Protestants whom fundamentalists believed were being corrupted by the intellectual and social developments of modernity. Fundamentalists fought against liberal theology, particularly the Christian socialism advocated by the Social Gospel movement.[5] But the fundamentalist revolt against a theology derived from social ethics (Tillich 1967, 303) was merely one part of their overarching rejection of modernity, which they perceived to be undermining the cultural and moral power of Christian faith. Higher biblical criticism, the scientific idea of evolution, and changes in gender roles all were targets of fundamentalist assaults (Marsden [1980] 1982; DeBerg 1990). When fundamentalists lost their battle for historic Christian institutions in the 1920s, they left and formed their own, though with little numerical success (Wuthnow 1988, 137).

The act that finally thrust fundamentalists into the public eye also signaled the collapse of fundamentalism's first wave. Deeming Darwin's evolutionary theories an affront to the creative powers of God, fundamentalists publicly sided against Tennessee high school teacher John T. Scopes at the notorious "monkey trial." Convicted of teaching evolutionary theory, Scopes lost his case legally but won it culturally. Evolutionary theory was mainstreamed into American public education, while fundamentalists slowly sank from public view (Balmer 1992; Wuthnow 1988, 135).[6]

Now, on the cusp of the third millennium, a second wave of fundamentalism is underway. It is this wave that Mount Olive and Bay Chapel ride. Though not a direct descendent of the original fundamentalists, some of whom are still around, second-wave Christian fundamentalists are both like and unlike their predecessors. First-wave fundamentalists stood out in stark contrast to the culture of their time and were often dismissed as outdated and irrelevant. Second-wave fundamentalists are sophisticated players in contemporary media culture and have become adept at promoting a culturally current public image (Hadden and Shupe 1988; Fitzgerald [1981] 1986). Where first-wave fundamentalists were among the least politicized groups in the country, second-wave fundamentalists are politically active and savvy (Fitzgerald [1981] 1986). Although they strive to be less rigid ideologically than traditional fundamentalists (Hadden and Shupe 1988), second-wave fundamentalists, like first-wavers, espouse "rock hard certainties . . . against doctrinal drift and confusion" (Bendroth 1993, 5), and gender remains a prominent issue for them (DeBerg 1990; Bendroth 1993, 11–12). They decry the ordination of women, and laud an energized masculinity. Bill McCartney's Promise Keepers, headquartered in Boulder, Colorado, is an outgrowth of the redirected masculinity these movements encourage (Bendroth 1993, 127). As in the first wave, evolutionary theory is deemed ungodly by second-wave fundamentalists, but they have organized special-purpose groups to promote the teaching of creationism in public schools (Wuthnow 1988, 190; Fitzgerald [1981] 1986, 130). As Harvey Cox once perceptively noted, fundamentalists who actively engage the culture seriously risk falling prey to the culture they criticize (Neuhaus and Cromartie 1987, 300). Yet the primary characteristic of second-wave fundamentalists is their strikingly bold willingness to undertake precisely this risk.

From the standpoint of the women I interviewed, the categorization is quite clear. When I asked female believers whether they considered themselves fundamentalist, the most frequent reply I received was, "That's what other people call me." Bay Chapel and Mount Olive women indicated that they are acknowledged as fundamentalists by those with whom they regularly come into contact. And they are content with that.

▨ *Research History and Method*

In academic literature, the involvement of contemporary women in the United States with male-dominated, conservative Christianity has been analyzed and interpreted alternately as antifeminist (Brown, in Hawley 1993; Einstein 1982; Wuthnow 1987; Himmelstein 1986) or postfeminist (Stacey 1990; Rosenfelt and Stacey 1987; Rapp 1988) social statements. To those outside Bay Chapel and Mount Olive, the women involved in these congregations can appear coopted, disingenuous. Perhaps this is because in traditional studies of Christian fundamentalism women are an object that fundamentalism frames. For my study, I wanted to invert this relationship. Thus, my research design, field work, analysis, and writing have been gynocentric, an exercise in women's standpoint theory (Smith 1990). I start by considering how fundamentalist congregations present themselves to female believers. Then, I step through the mirror and consider (to the extent it is epistemologically possible) how women who get involved with these congregations see themselves and why they come to structure their lives out of a committed interaction with a fundamentalist group. The result is that in much of what follows, the reader will encounter the relatively novel experience of learning how believing women frame Christian fundamentalism rather than the other way around.

Research for this book began out of a study, funded by the Lilly Endowment, of rapidly growing new Christian movements. For that project, I dedicated approximately twenty hours a week for two calendar years to studying the Calvary Chapel and Hope Chapel movements. Since I lived in southern California at the time, southern California congregations received the bulk of my attention; however, I also visited congregations in New York, New Mexico, and Kentucky and attended eight movement-wide events, where I interviewed conservative Christian pastors and dedicated lay adherents from across the United States, Australia, and western Europe. During these site visits, I conducted over one hundred unstructured, taped interviews with congregational participants and leaders that averaged an hour in length. I also prepared 140 sets of field notes, detailing a wide range of ceremonies, meetings, and events sponsored by each movement.

When the project ended, I began a second study focused on women's participation in the Calvary Chapel and Hope Chapel movements. I selected as case studies two congregations as case studies whose demographics and size recommended them as typical of the rapidly growing new Christian groups.

To protect their privacy, I refer to these two congregations throughout the book as Mount Olive (the Calvary Chapel congregation) and Bay Chapel (the Hope Chapel reform congregation).

My relationship to the people at these congregations was a cordial one. At the project's inception, I identified myself to the pastoral leadership of Bay Chapel and Mount Olive as an academic researcher interested in women's religiosity. Their senior pastors readily introduced me to key women leaders who proved to be accessible and cooperative throughout my entire study. Over the course of the six months, I generated eighty-nine sets of field notes, covering at least one session of every Bible study, retreat, and other activity advertised in congregational bulletins as being for women only, as well as a variety of congregational events advertised as being open to all. After two months of field immersion, I enlisted the assistance of Mount Olive and Bay Chapel women to develop an interview guide. I subsequently used that guide to conduct semistructured interviews averaging two hours in length with forty-seven female believers: twenty-four at Bay Chapel and twenty-three at Mount Olive.

I chose the initial interviewees using a snowball approach. As I attended various events, I met and got to know fundamentalist women, some of whom I asked to interview for my research. After an interview, these women would later introduce me to other believing women, some of whom I interviewed as well. Midway through interviewing, I halted the snowball approach and selected the remaining interviewees intentionally, addressing imbalances that had developed in the interview pool. No one woman, or even all of them taken together, can be said to authoritatively represent everyone involved with the female enclaves at these congregations; however, the interview pool included women whose racial, social, and economic profile spanned each congregation's range and whose enclave involvement ranged from lengthy (since its inception) to recent (within the last year) and from low (an average of one meeting per month) to high (an average of one visit per week). All were involved with both general congregational activities and with the women's ministry programs of their congregations. Every interview was tape recorded (audio). I transcribed and coded all interview tapes myself.

▓ *Summary and Conclusions*

During the years I studied Christian fundamentalist congregations, every congregation I visited was covered by a relatively similar sacred canopy, bisected by a sacred gender wall, and had a sizable women's ministry program underway involving an average of 10 percent of all members. My conclusion is that women's ministries thrive in Christian fundamentalist congregations because they perform a necessary role: they empower women. Faced with the ubiquitous male dominance of overall congregational life, fundamentalist women establish a parallel symbolic world in which they can be fully contributing participants. When women's ministries are considered along with the rest of what Mount Olive and Bay Chapel offered to women— intense religiosity, free child care, free counseling, readily available community, lively music, emotive singing, affordable continuing education and inexpensive weekend retreats—the decision that some women make to be actively involved with a Christian fundamentalist congregation can seem a fairly rational choice. In addition, for some it is a particularly rational choice, because the congregation is their spouses' employer, and communal social pressures necessitate their presence.

For those interested in the history and cultural influence of American Christianity, there are sound theoretical reasons for paying close attention to developments within the religious groups that the "godly women" of Mount Olive and Bay Chapel have joined. Thirty years ago, neither of these congregations existed. Today, each regularly fills its physical plant with baby-boomer and baby-buster Christians and their offspring and some Generation X-ers as well. The two decades of growth each has experienced—and the fact that each is almost totally made up of relatively young adherents and their children—hints that these congregations (and others with similar demographics) are the sites where the prevailing practices and beliefs of American Protestantism in the next millennium will be determined.

The religiosity of female believers is of considerable theoretical relevance in this regard. Gender in the United States functions such that women have carried the dominant cultural responsibility for religious life since the 1800s (Douglas 1977). Feminist research into this phenomenon indicates that this holds true regardless of the religion involved. It is credible to surmise, then, that whether a religious group succeeds in the United States is largely dependent upon the extent to which it can attract and retain the support of women. Given Christian fundamentalist institutions' regressive treatment of women, this situation presents an especial challenge for them.

In contemplating the faith of fundamentalist women, it is important to note that while Jerry Falwell, Pat Robertson, and other men who have dominated the leadership of fundamentalist institutions have become nationally prominent figures, and the Promise Keepers had to enjoy only slight numerical success before garnering national media attention, Christian fundamentalist women and the huge ministries they manage (which dwarf men's ministries in size and have existed far longer) have remained invisible to the public eye. The pages that follow seek to rectify this imbalance by providing an outlet for Christian fundamentalist women's voices to be heard.

I concur with the assessment of James P. Wind and James W. Lewis of the extraordinary importance congregations studies offer for discerning the currents of American social and religious life (Wind and Lewis 1994). Placed on the human social body at its warmest, congregations are religious thermometers that take the temperature of American existence. They are social sites where groups maintain particular values over time; thus, they are among the first places where change in the composition of public or private moralities become obvious. Especially given the increasing pluralism and uncertain homogenization of the American public, we need more extensive congregational studies examining how communities are living out their religious beliefs if we are ever to extend our understanding of the human religious impulses taking shape in the spiritual anagram of the United States.

As the chapters that follow disclose, the godly women of Bay Chapel and Mount Olive are dedicated to securing for themselves and their families a thoroughly religious, morally conservative life. To realize this goal, they invest themselves in fundamentalist congregations and then draw upon the symbolic resources they find and develop there to map out and assess their choices in life. Yet the considerable energy they devote to matters of faith is not solely dedicated to achieving personal ends. They channel some of it, as well, into traditional Christian practices such as feeding the hungry, clothing the naked, and visiting those in prison—although, as premillennialists, they undertake these activities more out of obedience than hope. Christian Penelopes in a postmodern world, the women of Mount Olive and Bay Chapel pass their days adoring God and laboring together for personal and societal holiness while they wait for Jesus to return.

Joining Up ❀ *CHAPTER 2*
Women and Fundamentalist Conversion

W hat motivates a well-educated, late twentieth-century American woman to join an intensely pious, world-reorienting Christian fundamentalist congregation whose life is centered around a single book and whose prevailing discourse on women, when compared to prevailing social norms, sounds, at best, reactionary? The reasons women give for the faith commitments they have made are as unique as their widely varying autobiographies; however, common sociological and socio-economic factors in the stories they tell about when and why they joined a fundamentalist congregation intimate that when an adult woman is confronted with unfortunate personal circumstances, the fault lines in contemporary gender practices can push her toward a highly restrictive religious commitment. Gender fault lines that left women notably vulnerable to personal trauma include high mobility and divorce rates, coupled with women's generally lower wages and typical shouldering of most of the responsibility for childrearing. As these factors combined, women found themselves profoundly needing the support of family or community, but often living far from where these resources were readily available to them. And so they would reach out.

To the women I interviewed, Mount Olive and Bay Chapel were the groups that most effectively responded. This is partly attributable to certain inherent sociological factors of Christian fundamentalism. The movement is inherently communal. To Christian fundamentalists, spiritual well-being is directly linked to the congregation. Generally, fundamentalists consider humanity as hapless, ensnared in a difficult, bleak existence from which it needs to be saved and brought into relationship with God; however, the concrete place where fundamentalists expect each other to exhibit their saved state, once it is underway, is in a Christian fundamentalist congregation. Thus becoming a fundamentalist entails more than accepting a canopy of sacred beliefs. It requires coming under that canopy's protection and abiding there, linking one's life to the community of believers it shelters. Having cast one's lot in with the group, one is expected to interact with it as the primary social network through which one's life values are determined.

At Bay Chapel and Mount Olive, those who join the congregation eventually are expected to to give a public testimony recounting the story of her/his salvation. This testimony of conversion situates the convert under the sacred canopy; the conversion story itself is a narrative home that others can "see" and subsequently visit. Importantly, the conversion story *is* a testimony. It publicly divulges the details of an experience in which the convert discovered the divine pattern that now organizes her/his life. Intrinsically motivational, a good conversion story reinforces the religious commitment of the person telling it while moving its audience toward analogous behavior.[1] Autobiographical in form, with rich descriptions of events in the life of the narrator, conversion stories have as their organizational center this rhetorical objective. Consequently, while the details of a conversion story are immensely personal, the story itself is inherently public. To withhold a conversion story is to deny the story's truth; therefore, to the extent that the concrete details of a person's life advance the rhetorical objective, they are included. Those that do not are scrupulously pruned.

Bay Chapel and Mount Olive women proved an inexhaustible source of conversion stories, willing to recount at great length and at any time or place how they acquired or had thrust upon them the faith that, for most, now encompassed the constitutive meaning of their existence.[2] The urgent desire that can propel believers to convey their conversion stories was vividly demonstrated to me during the first Bay Chapel women's retreat I attended. The retreat was held in Palm Beach and began on a Friday, in the early evening. Like most in attendance, I had about a two-hour drive to get to the retreat center where the weekend meeting was being held. Once I arrived, it took another thirty minutes or so for me to check in and find my room. I was feeling slightly tired when the opening session began, and those around did not appear to be feeling significantly more energized than I was. Before the session started, Ellen indicated to me that she would like to introduce me to the group, and I had agreed. Thus, I was not surprised when, midway through the opening welcome session, Ellen mentioned my name to the group and asked me to stand up—though I was a bit taken aback when she handed me the microphone and asked me to introduce myself. As briefly as I could, I described my research project and explained that I had come on the retreat to further my understanding of their faith. Then I quickly sat down. A few choruses later, the first formal retreat session began. It was on women's spirituality and lasted slightly over two hours. When it was over, I was exhausted and ready to call it a night; however, when I got up to leave the hall, I was besieged by women who wanted to talk about their faith. Since it was impossible to start any serious interviewing that night, I took down their names and then spent every spare minute I had over the next two days listening to their testimonies. I diligently tape-recorded interviews with more than twenty women, yet I was not able to get to all who wanted to testify. Mount Olive women were like Bay Chapel women in this regard. They did not merely agree to speak about their faith; they evangelistically pursued the opportunity. In focus meetings near the end of my field-work, Mount Olive and Bay Chapel women claimed that having an "on the record" opportunity to speak about conversion and faith was one of the best facets of my extended stay among them.

Congregational Factors of Conversion

The private/public duality of women's conversion stories mirror the private/public character of conversion that Mount Olive and Bay Chapel congregational practices encourage. As new congregations still in their first generation of leadership, neither Bay Chapel nor Mount Olive had inherited members; therefore, in the competitive American religion marketplace, each needed to attract new believers into their folds simply to survive. Because of this, both congregations were dependent upon and, perhaps not inconsequentially, dynamically organized around soliciting mature individuals to join the group. The centrality of conversion in Mount Olive and Bay Chapel congregational life was reinforced by the theology of salvation for the individual that the pastors at each espoused. It established the norms for the conversion process and shaped the "expectations and experiences of converts" (Rambo 1993, 173). In the religious worldview of Bay Chapel and Mount Olive, the conversion process constructed the bridge to salvation. It established a personal relationship with Jesus, with salvation being the on-going experience of the tie forged in that moment.[3]

Conversion of outsiders is a dominant aspect of the ministry of both churches, and the techniques by which each carries it out are quite similar. Near the end of each service, the presiding pastor issues an invitation for any present who want to know Jesus to come forward. At Mount Olive, those who come forward are required to repeat aloud a "sinner's prayer." At Bay Chapel, no rote confession is required; however, those who come forward are asked to pray aloud in front of the congregation along with the pastor. Once a person completes the public conversion performance, she or he is taken to a side room to speak privately with counselors about the significance of what has just happened and to receive pamphlets detailing congregational beliefs. To newcomers, the daily conversational practices at Bay Chapel and Mount Olive gradually provided a special dialect that could be drawn upon to describe their own conversion. The congregations offered special classes that schooled adherents in conversion conversation techniques. Believers were equipped with materials to pass out to potential converts and encouraged to attend training programs where they would be taught how to cultivate conversations with nonbelievers into becoming conversion events.

░ *Conversion or Reorientation?*

In their classic article on conversion, John Lofland and Rodney Stark defined it as, "When a person gives up one . . . perspective or ordered view of the world for another" (Lofland and Stark 1965, 862). In a footnote to this definition, they cautioned against what they contended were muddied uses of the word "conversion" to refer to arousal within a meaning system. Their contention was that "conversion" should be limited to the act of switching from one system to another. Customarily, Bay Chapel and Mount Olive women referred to the process of establishing their relationship-based faith as conversion; but, was it conversion in Lofland and Stark's sense? Beth had been associated with Mount Olive for nine years when I met her. She admitted that she considered herself a Christian and had participated in Christian rituals for years before her conversion; yet, she viewed the transformation she experienced when she established her relationship-based faith as substantive. To Beth, there was a crucial difference between "believing," which was what she had done in her earlier years in the church, and "accepting," which is what she did when she underwent the conversion process. Her belief had been to no avail. It was acceptance that brought what she described as a "metamorphosis." "I've only been a Christian for nine years . . . born again, Christian. I believed in the Lord, but as far as that metamorphosis that takes effect when you accept the Lord into your life as lord and savior, that began nine years ago. My life has slowly changed through the years since then. I'm still the same person; but my thoughts, my opinions, my contentment with myself is so different."

The majority of the women who got involved with Bay Chapel and Mount Olive were like Beth in that they were not new converts at all; thus, in some ways the term "conversion" may overstate the amount of socioreligious change involved (Lofland and Stark 1965). Most had a history of involvement in Christianity prior to conversion (19 of 24 at Mount Olive; 19 of 23 at Bay Chapel), though they frequently described this involvement as minimal.[4] Only one woman, reared an "atheist-Buddhist" in Thailand, described herself as possessing a worldview substantially at odds with Christian beliefs before her new affiliation. Yet all of the women, like Beth, considered what they had experienced as a conversion, a substantial change in the spiritual, emotional, and mental pattern of their lives. Each associated current faith commitments with a qualitatively different world view and a transformed lifestyle.

Given the high degree of correspondence between the prior

and present religious attachments of my interviewees, Lofland and Stark's concept of "reorientation" holds some explanatory appeal (Lofland and Stark 1965, 862). As they converted, women positioned themselves anew within the meaning system of Christianity—a religion to which most had been exposed in childhood. In spite of the descriptive benefit "reorientation" offers, acknowledging as it does the tie between the women's past and present religious involvement, it would be a misleading term to use in this case. It would relativize the amount of change in the women's lives that the conversion process stimulated and unwarrantedly contradict as well the rationale they offered for their own behaviors. Obviously, testimonies of new believers that totally discount prior religious experiences have to be held somewhat suspect, since the formulaic nature of conversion stories requires a convert to problematize her or his past (Ellwood 1973). All conversion stories necessarily interpret preconversion life based on postconversion beliefs (Gordon 1984, 43; Berger and Luckmann 1967, 159–160). However, later self-evaluations of one's earlier circumstances are not necessarily misleading. They can be more accurate, based on additional information. It can indeed be the case that one was once lost and now is found. Bay Chapel and Mount Olive converts were heavily involved in groups and programs that were, to them, new. I visited women in their homes, met their spouses, talked with their children, and sometimes had coffee with their neighbors. Over the entire course of this study, I found little dissonance between the stories of life change women told me and the observable features of their lives. As women got involved with Mount Olive and Bay Chapel and the women's ministry programs they offered, their ideas, their friendships, their marriages, and even their self-images substantially altered. In view of this, I contend that the women I interviewed employed conversionist language to describe what occurred to them because the process they underwent was indeed conversion.[5] Joining these congregations dramatically reorganized the way they understood themselves and their lives (Berger 1963). They became "total converts," who enacted their faith in words and deeds (Lofland and Stark 1965, 864). Though their new meaning system incorporated many of the symbols of a familiar religious faith, these women were converted.[6] Intrafaith conversion could also be construed as a highly rational choice: it is a maximizing behavior that allows believers to "conserve on the value of their previous religious investments" (Iannaccone 1995, 14).

Conversion as Process

The women of Bay Chapel and Mount Olive told long, engaging, graphic, and often painful stories of how and why they got involved in relationship-based faith. Although examining these stories as a whole elides the unique aspects of each woman's experience, comparisons among them reveal certain consistent factors. Throughout the array of their conversion stories, conversion was always described as a kaleidoscope of multiple and varying experiences rather than as repeated articulations of a central, definable act. Many, though not all, did include a salvation event—an initial public testimony or realization—but conversion, the transformation of self, took place over considerable time. Conversion was a process, not an event. Because of this, the use of the single word "conversion" to categorize the stories of how each came to understand herself in a Christian context is more a helpful subterfuge than a totalizing capsulation. It consistently masks meaningful details while making major overarching observations possible.

Although dominant themes were present in conversion stories, each narrative remained stubbornly unique, a spiritual journey embedded in the particularities of an individual life. Where comparisons exposed commonalities among the women's stories and indicated that wider social forces abetted conversion, the individual decisions each woman made that got her involved with Bay Chapel or Mount Olive were unfailingly personal. This was, in fact, one of the most arresting features revealed by a comparison of conversion stories: their consistent individuality. In their conversion stories, the women recounted personal considerations as the factors that stimulated their conversion process. Family, health, substance abuse, spiritual restlessness—the reasons themselves varied. Their personalness did not. For Mount Olive and Bay Chapel women, the nonacknowledgment of structural factors in their conversion was a structural factor of conversion tales. In the conversion story, the personal was personal. It was not until after the salvation event, the "Aha!" moment within the conversion process, that cultural or societal factors were ever acknowledged in the story. When they were, they were portrayed as a chaos that originated from the disconnection of culture and society from God's order for the world.

In the conversion stories of the Mount Olive and Bay Chapel women, the preconversion self was seen as an individual circumscribed in knowledge and vision. No woman told a conversion story that featured her as in possession of a keen, analytic overview of the congregation or her fellow converts. No woman described herself as evaluating Bay Chapel or Mount Olive to discern whether roles for women were limited or not. They commonly described conversion as a process. Neither instant nor absolute, it generally occurred in stages spread out over years and gave their life a center and boundaries. To Bay Chapel and Mount Olive women, conversion unfolded. Though intriguing similarities appeared among their conversion stories, the stories fit Lewis Rambo's definition of conversion: they were highly varied, nonideal narratives, each of which described a "process of religious change" (Rambo 1993, 5).

In their narratives, women depicted conversion as a historical drama that occurred in three acts: preconversion, the salvation event, and postconversion.[7] The first act, preconversion, included everything that occurred before public commitment. It began with a description of early childhood family life and was followed by a nonprogressive, chronologically arranged narrative of subsequent events that alternated between development and dissolution of the self. In the way women related this narrative, it often was organized around and pointing toward the triggering event that sparked conversion. Like many believing women, Cheryl, at Mount Olive, reached back into childhood to start the preconversion stage of her story.

> I was brought up with basic good morals, right and wrong, and a strong family concept; but, as far as the organized church, no. My life changed from knowing there was something missing in it. I just knew there was something missing, something I needed. We were a close family. We did things together. But there was just something I wanted. I felt the drawing to go to church. If people aren't Christian, they don't understand that, but I know now that the Spirit was drawing me there. It was an emotional feeling from within, a desire of my heart.

Most, like Cheryl, described themselves as having had little or no involvement in religious events or activities in early life, though some religious interest; yet, as mentioned above, many were not without religious history. Roughly one-fourth of the women at Bay Chapel and one-third of the women at Mount Olive described the preconversion period of their lives as a time marked by heavy religious involvement (8 of 24 at Mount Olive; 6 of 23 at Bay Chapel); most were at best mildly involved.[8]

The preconversion religious affiliation of women varied. The most frequently mentioned was Roman Catholicism (8 of 23 at Bay Chapel; 7 of 24 at Mount Olive).[9] The varieties of Baptists taken together placed a distant second (5 of 23 at Bay Chapel; 2 of 24 at Mount Olive). Yet the prior religious involvement, whether minimal or significant, whether Catholic, Baptist, or something else, fell short of meeting the woman's religious needs. Josie, a forty-three-year-old Mexican-American Bible study leader at Mount Olive, spoke of the personal turmoil she experienced as she slowly came to realize the extent to which her former religious involvement had failed her. "I met a girl-friend who always seemed full of joy. I thought, her family's a lot like mine. How does she do it? When I told her my hus-band and I were splitting up, she asked me if I would go to her church. I [went and] started hearing how the Lord loved me, how he meant for good things to happen in my life. It was pain-ful, bitter, sad to me that I couldn't hear that message in Ca-tholicism. Where I would have loved to find the answer, the messages were not coming through."

The second act of the conversion narrative was the salva-tion event, the time when an active, public commitment to relationship-based faith was made. This salvation event trans-formed the personal story, for salvation in the form of a rela-tionship with Jesus was the narrative climax. Once it was introduced, it functioned as the source of cohesive meaning for the earlier as well as the later events portrayed in the narra-tive. Development and dissolution of the self continued after the salvation event, but they were subordinated to the over-riding center of cohesive meaning, a relationship with Jesus. The salvation event, as women described it, followed Lofland's pattern in that it was portrayed as initiated by a religious inci-dent that culminated in public testimony. During conversion, the woman moved to a different understanding of herself in re-lation to ultimate values and truths.

Irene's happened unexpectedly, when she went to the beach with a friend one afternoon and stumbled upon a Bay Chapel baptism service.

I went to the beach with a friend of mine, and they were having a baptism down there. Mike was there [baptizing people].
I knew at that moment, I'd found a strong calling, that the Lord
wanted me to be baptized. I brought no clothing whatsoever
to change into, but I just went ahead and did it. Pastor Mike
was the one who baptized me. It was the first Mount Olive
event I attended, and I got baptized. I was twenty-one at that
time.

Jane's public commitment was triggered by the religious healing of a physical injury. It took place at a Mount Olive musical
concert.

I was sitting on the front row [at the concert]. I had just that
summer gone through knee surgery, and later had my knee
faith-healed through a pastor at Calvary Chapel, Bakersfield.
So I went forward and accepted the Lord. I was totally over-
come with the deepest peace I have ever had in my entire
life—knowing that if I were to leave that auditorium that
evening and be shot in the head by some maniac, I'd immediately be with Jesus. That was the peace he had given me. My
life has been totally different since.

Maria, a Mount Olive regular, described her salvation event not
as something that involved public testimony but as a revela-
tion inspired by disgust with her own substance abuse. It
changed her life.

My girlfriend and I were both tired of our lives not changing.
I was twenty-two and got tired of it [alcohol and drug abuse].
She heard about Mount Olive from somebody and took me
there. I sat in the church with my mouth open, listening to
the pastor and saying, "This is out of the Bible?" I couldn't
believe it. I had never been a Bible student. I didn't know these
words coming from the Bible. I was amazed. I was thrilled. My
life changed at that point.

Postconversion, the shaking-out period following public testimony, was the third act of a typical conversion narrative. It was described as two or three progressive stages of involvement, each of which strengthened the imaginative grasp faith commitments had on a woman's sense of self and expanded the range of her life activities over which the language, symbols, and values of faith held sway.[10] Since my interviewees were in midadulthood, the postconversion phase of their stories rarely covered more than ten years. During this phase, the ramifications of the conversion process become evident. Though significant events occurred in the postconversion phase, neither Bay Chapel nor Mount Olive women characterized them as possessing vital motive power. The source of new energy resided solely in the saving connection with the new source of cohesive meaning, their relationship with Jesus. Amy, a young Asian-American member of Bay Chapel (her mother is Chinese, her father Thai) who had been a Christian for four years, described the transformation her conversion occasioned as one of perception. "I think for someone to really understand it—if they were saved, I think the light bulb would just go on suddenly. Because God is so real to you all of a sudden, whereas before he was like an idol. He was just hanging, you know? Like there was a cross and Jesus was lying there, that's kind of what you felt God was. Now, he's *real*. Do you know what I'm saying? Now, God is God."

Motivating Themes for Conversion

Two themes dominated the initial phase of the conversion stories the forty-seven women I interviewed told me. The most frequent was personal life crisis. Twenty-five women described themselves as being in a state of personal life crisis immediately prior to their salvation event (13 of 24 women at Mount Olive; 12 of 23 women at Bay Chapel). The second most fre-

TABLE 1	*Preconversion Conditions Cited in Women's Conversion Narratives*		
	Life crisis	*Marital-related life crisis (divorced)*	*Quest*
Mount Olive	13	10 (5)	7
Bay Chapel	12	8 (4)	7

quent theme was a growing awareness of personal emptiness combined with a desire for growth (7 of 24 at Mount Olive; 7 of 23 at Bay Chapel).[11] Sometimes the two themes overlapped, as in Kris's story. A twenty-three-year-old graduate of the University of Southern California and an Asian American member of Bay Chapel, guilt over her lifestyle resulted in her unexpectedly getting involved in a religious event on campus.

> One day I was walking by Tommy Trojan. They had all these booths there. I felt like I needed to . . . I felt like God was right and the things I was doing were wrong. So I went up to the booth. When I got up there I told them I wanted to know God. I remember I went back and told my boyfriend, and he laughed at me. Then . . . since I wasn't in any kind of fellowship, it was a one-day thing, and that was the end of it. I didn't even grow or get into the Word or know anything about it, but it was still nagging me. I thought, I want to know more about God. I want to know what he has to say, what he thinks of certain things.

While Kris did not immediately convert, the memory of that day stayed with her. Within six months, she was involved with Bay Chapel.

Usually, however, the women depicted themselves either as in a personal crisis prior to conversion or as in a heightened state of desire for personal change, rarely both. The common element between the two was the inability of existing physical, cognitive, emotional, and symbolic resources to meet an existential need, either to abate the crisis or to abet growth. Only one demographic factor distinguished women in one group from the other. This was the chronological age of the woman when the initial conversion experience transpired. Women who identified desire for personal growth as their preconversion motivating factor generally had an initial conversion experience in their late teens or early twenties. Women who identified personal crises as a motivational factor generally experienced an initial conversion in their mid- to late thirties.

The preconversion crises described to me universally stemmed from nuclear family issues. Sometimes the death of a parent, child, or other immediate family member precipitated the crisis. More frequently, the woman was having serious relational troubles with a primary male partner, almost always a spouse. Of the twenty-five personal-crisis stories, eighteen had marital crisis as their central theme, ranging from impending to actual separation and divorce (see table 1). Peggy explained, "My husband and I had a period in our marriage where it wasn't really good. It was much more bad than it was good, basically. Church became a refuge. It was a sanctuary. It was a safe place where people were glad to see me." Nine of the women who indicated that they were experiencing severe marital difficulties when they got involved with Bay Chapel or Mount Olive did divorce their spouses either immediately prior to or soon after their conversion. The other nine reconciled with their estranged spouses. In two cases these reconciliations involved remarrying a divorced spouse.

Nancy's story is both typical and atypical in this regard. A thirty-nine-year-old Bay Chapel member, Nancy described her conversion process as something she herself initiated in response to marital and family calamities. A believing aunt and friend also influenced her.

During the course of my marriage and towards the latter part of it, there was a systematic dissolving of every stable base in my life. My parents got divorced. My marriage was on the rocks. My job was gone.

I started reaching out to Christians I knew, picking up the New Testament my aunt had given to me for graduation. I was mentally or emotionally slowly coming to that point of going, "God you're the one that's in charge. Not me." But, I didn't want to take that step.

I associated being born again with being a Jesus freak and being mind-controlled. Not your own person. Something. It just didn't appeal, mainly from a pride standpoint. That fundamental issue of who's in charge of my life. Am I ultimately in charge of my life? Can I ultimately make things happen? Or, am I going to submit to God and he's going to be in charge—whatever that relationship meant.

As near as I can tell, this little light bulb went on in my head. My marriage is such a mess, and that's the most important thing to me in my life. I don't want this thing to end. God is the only one that can put it back together. I was totally convinced that he could do that. So, I called up this girlfriend of mine who I had a slightly nodding acquaintance with, and I go, "I want to get born again. I want to come pray with you." She was the most shocked person, because I was the only person she ever led to the Lord. When I look back, I guess it was kind of, uh, a caesarian rebirth instead of a natural one. I said, "I'm dedicating my life to the Lord."

For Nancy and other crisis-motivated converts, the conversion story empowered the self as well as others. It allowed converts to assign a purpose to the preconversion traumas they had experienced: these sufferings had thrust the self toward God.

▩ *Sex and Money*

To decipher the significance of a woman's conversion to fundamentalist Christianity, the cultural intersections of gender and religion in the United States must be taken into account. As historian Ann Braude acerbically has summed it up, "In America, women go to church" (Braude 1995, 7). Women receive more positive social sanctions for religious participation than men (DeBerg 1990, 22–23; Cott 1977, 199). From mainstream Christianity to reform Judaism, women make up the majority of believers, even though men dominate religious authority (Cornwall 1989; Batson, Schoenrade, and Ventis 1993; Braude 1995). If American religion were imaginatively conceptualized as a clothing store, two-thirds of its floor space would house garments for women; the manager's office would be occupied almost exclusively by men.

The historical bias favoring female involvement in religion in the United States is fostered by systemic imbalances between the sexes. An important one is in the area of economics. Paid less than men in all occupational categories and engaged in fulltime employment less often than men, women overall have lower direct access to disposable wealth than men (Banner 1992). Given their lower direct access to income, women's ability to actualize themselves is more circumscribed then men's. As a result, more American women than men may end up actualizing themselves in a religious group (Iannaccone 1990). Quite simply, religious groups offer them a more economically feasible way to achieve self-transformation and self-fulfillment than the culture in general does.

This bias is sharpened when women face life problems. While all men and women encounter at least a few problems in life, when women encounter them they do so with less disposable wealth to address them than men do. This imbalance may further steer women toward religion, because of the three principal avenues to address life problems supported in American society—politics, psychiatry, and religion (Lofland and Stark 1965)—religion is the cheapest. Religious products, from worship services to counseling sessions, are offered by most congregations either at a nominal charge or for free. The disparity between women's and men's disposable income makes the cost associated with any activity (including a religious one), while an important consideration for both, more important for women than for men. As a result, women are more structurally susceptible than men to religion's price advantage.[12] Thus, in the United States religion can be an attractive social commitment for women. It satisfies societal expectations traditionally associated with female gender roles. It provides a place to reconstruct the self without the economic cost of consumerism. It offers services that women with problems may need at a price they can afford.

An unemployed devotee of Mount Olive gave me my first clue about how cost can be a factor in women's religious involvement, and served as well to warn me against limiting the concept of cost too strictly to the monetary realm. Responding to a query about what, if anything, inspired her involvement with Mount Olive, Beth, who had converted after her sister's early death, explained, "I'm the person who gets the benefit from all this. I can go there, free of charge, be a part of this organization—God's family. I don't have to open my mouth. I don't have to do anything. I don't even have to contribute. I can sit there and watch all this stuff going on. You do that long enough and the next thing you know, you're walking with the flow." Beth's comments disclose how misleading it can be to confine an understanding of costs to any single meaning system. To Beth, cost factors ranged from monetary (i.e., the absence of any price of admission) to existential (i.e., the lack of any requirement that she personally contribute to public rituals). The poetic ideas and emotive music offered by Mount Olive were affective benefit agents that aroused Beth's conversion experience, but their low contingent cost factors influenced her response as well.

In spite of this, only one woman attributed her preconversion crisis to an economic issue (loss of job). Since most were employed at least part-time and none were independently wealthy, the absence of substantial comment on the contribution of economic factors made to preconversion crises was notable. I was not able to operationalize and test any theory regarding this absence; however, I did arrive at two, admittedly speculative, possibilities. One was gender-neutral. The taboo in American culture against discussing personal financial matters may well have been at work in this reticence. A second possibility was gender-related. At Bay Chapel and Mount Olive, economic worth, when discussed, was a value associated with men. The economic worth of women was largely absent from congregation rhetoric. The possibility that remunerative work might be a substantive source of personal fulfillment for women was not part of the public value system of either congregation. On the rare occasions when women's for-pay work was addressed in pastoral sermons or in discussions among members, such work was characterized as a misfortune sporadically forced upon women in order to help support their families. Because overall congregational values treated economic concerns as marginal to women, they would have been a questionable trope for women to include as a central motivating force in their conversion narratives. Its dissonance with the faith-centered, gender-bifurcated religious world of their congregation might have distracted listeners from the religious message they were attempting to convey and lessened its persuasive impact.[13]

⬚ *Cathy's Story*

Because of the insistent personalness that marked women's conversion stories, the taste and feel of conversion narratives are most accurately discerned through the lens of an individual life. To explore conversion in this way, in the particular, allows it the singularity that characterizes the genre. Cathy's conversion story, which follows, is unique. A tragedy sparked Cathy's conversion: the disappearance and death of her eldest child. A horror beyond belief, the event smashed Cathy's world and set her off on an excruciatingly intense search for meaning. Every event Cathy includes in the story she tells about her conversion is a critical nerve fiber of spiritual autobiography. The tripartite organizational principle of her story, including its preconversion, innocent, Edenic beginning that ends in dissolution and shattering despair, its midpoint salvation event, and the presumed stability of its conclusion, in which Cathy has a firm hold on religious wisdom, represents the form well.

I met Cathy at a Bay Chapel women's Bible study and interviewed her at her upscale, middle-class, southern California home in the fall of 1993. Cathy actually looks like the increasingly misleading, media-constructed image of a typical California female: she is white, blue-eyed, blonde, and though thirty-seven at the time, looked to be in her midtwenties at most. Her body was slim and tanned from years of surfing. Like the majority of women converts, Cathy described her conversion as the result of a religious quest set off by a personal life crisis.

The first stage of her story began with preconversion events. She told me she came from a family of thirteen children and had been reared a Catholic. When I asked about her work history, Cathy told me, "First of all, I got pregnant when I was sixteen and married Mike . . . so that gives you a little foundation right there." Twenty-one years and three children later, Cathy and Mike remain married. Cathy explained, "I've really done whatever I needed to do throughout the years to supplement our income and work around the kids' schedules so I wasn't gone all the time." Cathy had hoped to start her own business once their children were in school. She laid these hopes aside when her husband became desperate to do something other than drive a bread truck for a living. "He was always very frustrated. But since we started so young with a family, he was locked in. One day he came home and said, 'I can't do this. When I turn forty or fifty, I'll lose my mind. I've got to go back to school and do something else.'" Mike went to law school and eventually became a lawyer. Cathy worked at various times as a waitress, a receptionist, and a retail sales clerk to support the family while Mike pursued his studies.

A family tragedy set off Cathy's conversion process. She said, "I hadn't been working since the end of November. I'd had a major, major tragedy in my life." Cathy and Mike's eighteen-year-old daughter Sherry had gone to visit friends the day after Thanksgiving and had not returned. As events unfolded, Cathy and Mike started to think that their daughter probably had been murdered. But at first, all they knew was that she was gone. When Cathy and Mike were informed of Sherry's disappearance, the two responded quite differently. "My husband just went, 'She's gone. It's not good. I have to go to work.' You know, he just could not handle it. For me, I just had to do everything humanly possible as a mother to find out what had happened to my child." Cathy set up a mini-industry of family, neighbors, and friends doing what could be done to search for definite information about Sherry's disappearance. In spite of this, she got no concrete leads.

In her conversion story, Cathy depicted her suffering during this time as physically incapacitating. Pain was an active virus that attacked and ate away the patterns that structured her identity. To Cathy, the shock of losing her daughter shredded the meaning web by which she had lived. "I was just ready to check out. I had gone from being superwoman to, all of a sudden, just going down with it. I couldn't get out of bed anymore. I didn't have the strength to keep fighting. I was just starting to give up." Under pressure from family and friends, Cathy eventually abandoned the physical quest for her daughter's body. She had to accept that her daughter was dead. In her narrative, Cathy claimed that once her former life shattered she was incapable of forming anything new. "Everything I've ever done revolved around my family. I chose at a very early age to make a commitment to that. When I decided to do it, I did it 100 percent. Then to have everything I'd always worked for— and everything that was important to me was family—to have that shattered in a phone call. I just didn't have the strength to pick up the pieces and start to reform my life."

At this point, Cathy's conversion narrative shifted from preconversion, with its tropes of dissolution, into the early stages of the salvation event itself. Slowly, she initiated a religious quest for meaning, a search for a way to accept, to integrate, to go on from what had occurred. "I was always afraid of really knowing too much about God and committing my life to him 'cause I really didn't know what it involved, and I really didn't want to give anything up . . . have it be anything too weird or intense, or change and have my whole family think I was weird, or whatever. And all of a sudden I thought—it was like this voice saying, 'You were always too afraid to do this.' And I thought, Right now I'm too afraid not to do it." She began her search by praying privately, but discovered neither answers nor comfort in prayer. Then, she sought a religious community. She initially attempted to return to the Roman Catholic community she'd drifted away from in early adulthood. "I went inside of the church. It was like the same church I had grown up in. The oak and varnish smelt the same. I even saw a couple of the same faces that were older. But it was just la-la-la, da-da-da. You know. When he gave his sermon, it was very empty. I went up and received communion, and I came and sat back down. I remember feeling, 'Is this it? Is this what I'm supposed to fall back on?'"

Cathy's salvation event transpired over a two-day period, outside the congregational setting. She described it as a frightening experience that life events flung her into rather than as an option over which she exercised any control. It began with what she metaphorically depicts as a leap of faith while praying with her cousin Mary.

I felt like I was jumping off a cliff, but I was already going down anyway, so I had nothing to lose. I jumped off thinking, If you can just slow down my fall a little, Lord, and be there a little, and give me a little faith, whatever that is, and just let me be in touch with you a little and have what some other people around me have that makes them look like they do better than me, or they have more answers, or more peace, that will maybe give me some energy to keep going a little while longer. I felt good, as if I'd made a decision or a commitment, and that felt good. I left Mary's house feeling good, a little lighter and more like I knew where my daughter was. But it wasn't like *salvation*. I just felt a little better—that it was good to visit with Mary, that she really helped me.

The next morning, I woke up and said to my husband, "It's a beautiful day out. I want to go to the beach." For three months, I couldn't have told you if it was foggy or sunny. To actually acknowledge that it was a pretty day and that I might want to spend it outside was, like, an amazing thing to me. I wasn't dead anymore. It was wonderful, but it was a little bit scary. It was like, *man*, what happened and what did I commit to? What is going on here? I thought, This isn't possible. I feel full of joy right now. I have peace. I feel his compassion, and I felt like he gave me this message, like he had been with me all the time. I just hadn't known he was there. It was like I was Dorothy in *The Wizard of Oz*. At the end, she finds out there's no place like home. She had the power in the shoes the whole time and didn't know it. That's how I felt.

It was only after making this connection that Cathy got involved with Bay Chapel. There, she found symbol systems, rituals, and experiences of community that mediated a religious experience powerful enough to carry her through the tremendous loss she had endured. As she explained in a brief postconversion coda, Cathy did not think of herself as perfected by what had happened to her: "I still do things wrong, just like anybody else. We're all in the same boat. But I just think the closer you keep to God's will, the better off you're gonna be and the safer that is for a lot of reasons, you know?" Although Cathy does not claim that conversion will protect her against future tragedy, the inference is clear. The closer one adheres to God's will, the better off one will be. And whom or what did she find that satisfied her desire to be aligned with God's will? The teachings and community of a Christian fundamentalist congregation.

In its full two-hour run, Cathy's conversion story is marked by profoundly intimate details of loss and intense torment. The personalness of her misery makes it uniquely a story of Cathy's life. Nevertheless, it is also true that the influence of twentieth-century American culture can be discerned in many of its elements. For instance, the narratives long introspective passages assume an interest in "the psychology of the convert" and invite a psychological reading (Brereton 1994). This contrasts with pre–twentieth-century American conversion narratives, which drew heavily upon biblical texts for content. The preconversion phase of Cathy's story, like the preconversion stories of most Mount Olive and Bay Chapel female believers, revealed critical fault lines in middle-class American gender roles. It disclosed the relationship between economics and the fragile sites of human identity. During the most intense periods of the family crisis, Mike's work gave him a place away from the family where he could sublimate his pain. Like most employed American males confronted with a life crisis, Mike, who worked full-time outside the home, was pushed by that work experience to "get on with it" and curtail his grief (Rando 1986, 26). Cathy, whose life energies were centered on family—for whom work was at best a secondary value—possessed no equivalent haven or stimulus, a situation typical of adult American women (Hagestad 1984, 38). When tragedy struck, Mike had meaningful activities with which he could space out his pain and an institutional impetus for its closure. Cathy, with neither, stayed in agony—thereby triggering the conversion process that transformed her into a godly woman.

Theological signs of modernity were evident in Cathy's narrative as well. She never spoke of a conviction of sin. She did not interpret her daughter's disappearance and death as warranted by sin—hers, her husband's, or their daughter's. Guilt was not evident in Cathy's story, nor a God of judgment. She did not mention hell or cry out to God for the damnation of those responsible for her daughter's abduction and probable murder. She also expressed no concern with theodicy. In this, Cathy exemplified my interviewees: none blamed themselves, society, or God for the crises they experienced. They were not events attributed to human depravity or a judgment-seeking deity but were presented as awful events that simply happened. Hell within women's stories was the internal, psychological trauma provoked by devastating events. Hell was not a place one might be consigned to after death. It was "interior . . . found in the ordinary world" (Brereton 1991, 51).

In her conversion narrative, Cathy, like all my interviewees, described her preconversion life and troubles as this-worldly. For Cathy, the preconversion period was one of desperate horror, during which she fought to live through the known and unknown events surrounding the disappearance of her oldest child. For others, the preconversion phase was a time when they were confronted with fragmenting relationships (as was Nancy), unanticipated deaths, or surprising health problems.

Yet in each crisis-motivated conversion, the response women made to crisis was to begin an intense, poignant search for meaning, for symbolic or textual messages or an experience of human community that worked. The result was that each became a godly woman.

※ *Summary and Conclusions*

The religious outlook of the conversion narratives of Bay Chapel and Mount Olive women is in decided contrast to American middle-class consumerism, which depicts conversion of the self as something that occurs through purchasing a product. Overtly Christian in language and theological in structure, these narratives present conversion as a process that offers a Buddhist-like release from suffering that is a byproduct of a new relationship with God.

Once converted, then, it should come as no surprise that these women insisted that what they were interested in was "not religion, but a relationship." Yet this tenet encourages believers to discount the role congregations play in making their "relationship" with Jesus ideologically, emotionally, and experientially possible. Fundamentalist conversational practices as well as the organization of congregational life, while determinant factors in conversion narratives, were seldom identified by the narrators as pivotal elements of their conversion process. If, as Gertrude Stein once asserted, language does not alter because it "is an altar," which prescribes what it describes (Stein 1928, 108), it is not surprising to discover that Bay Chapel and Mount Olive women evaluated the success of their conversion processes on the basis of their ability to experience and sustain relationship-based faith.

Taking into consideration the American macro-bias favoring women's participation in religion along with the pervasive domination of congregational authority and leadership by men (see chapter 3), it is a small step to codify the women of Bay Chapel and Mount Olive as culturally constructed consumers of religious goods over which men hold a production monopoly. For many of the women I interviewed, the initial part of this assessment is apt. Most got involved with these groups as Cathy did, in the midst of life crises to which cultural gender norms left them peculiarly vulnerable. And these same gender norms were at play as they combed through public and private resources for spiritual, physical, and emotional assistance. To those who converted, the most accessible, affordable, meaningful, emotionally satisfying assistance they encountered was lodged in a conservative Protestant Christian congregation. But it would be inaccurate to characterize them only as consumers. A central argument of this book is that the women of Bay Chapel and Mount Olive create as well as consume religious products, especially at the congregational level (again, see chapter 3).

On what recurrently were circuitous routes to conversion, the stories of my interviewees were marked by the painful impact of social flux in late twentieth-century life.[14] Mixed marriages, high divorce rates, unstable gender roles, and complex emotional ties were the external challenges women faced, while perceiving themselves as bearing the brunt of societal expectations to nurture and sustain their "fluid, postmodern families" (Stacey 1990) was a primary internal hurdle. Although women's conversion narratives were inundated with the pressures and patterns of social life, the stories responded to this condition unreflectively until after the salvation event. For many of the women, the conversion process was a bridge that spanned potentially dangerous meaning gaps in life.

Women's conversion narratives psychologically construct for them a certain freedom. In an analysis of women's conversion narratives from 1800 to the present, Brereton speculates that when women name a divine figure such as Jesus Christ as the unconditional center of their lives, it "suggests the creation of at least a small space of one's own . . . if not a room of one's own" (Brereton 1991, 94). For women, conversion brought healing and strategic empowerment from the subsequent involvement in congregational life that expanded their sense of personal agency. Bay Chapel and Mount Olive rituals mediated powerful religious experiences that helped godly women cope with the oppression and pain that marred their lives.

Though driven by cultural issues, women's conversion stories cannot meaningfully be reduced to them. After all, countless women suffer life traumas, but only a few become godly women. The unique vagaries of each woman's life—her individual strengths and preferences, kinship networks, religious history, racial/ethnic identifiers, and so on—affected how powerfully each aspect of modernity shaped or limited her, played a role in influencing the appeal various cultural alternatives might have. Then, of course, there is always the mystery of the Spirit. It drew them, the women said, to make the choices they did. The form of conversion narrative that thrived among these women was a tale in which the self was devastated, then transformed. Importantly, the transformation of self was not identified as a product of the self. It was achieved by God, the Creator. In this sense, these conversion stories go against the American dream, which favors stories of self-wrought achievement. Apart from God, the only thing Bay Chapel and Mount Olive women claimed to have achieved was personal devastation. It was only in relationship with God and through the considerable support of their congregation and its female enclaves that these women experienced a quality of life that made it possible for them to endure.

The Hand That Rocks the Cradle

CHAPTER 3

Authority and Power in Congregational Life

"The hand that rocks the cradle rules the world"—this paradoxical proverb about who controls the human community is a heuristic device that I use to call attention to the pervasive irony that characterized the authority and power of women at Bay Chapel and Mount Olive. With undertones of humor, the saying—from a poem by William Ross Wallace (1819–1891)—asserts that the people who rule the world are those who nurture infants. By this, it implies that infant nurture is a world-shaping task. This is a position with which conservative Protestant ideology, with its emphasis on family values, largely agrees. Yet two subtler implications adumbrated by this trope are the ones most pertinent to Bay Chapel and Mount Olive women. One is the implication that people remote from the domain of public authority can achieve social control of the group. The other, typically projected into the refrain by readers, is that those who achieve such remote control are likely to be women (since women, historically, have been responsible for rearing infants), while those who publicly rule, but are not actually in charge, will be men. Incidents that occurred during my field studies of Mount Olive and Bay Chapel revealed that in these congregations both hold true.

Through a contrast of appearance with reality, the proverb asserts that if you take humanity's power structures at face value you commit a cardinal error. You confuse authority, or positions of leadership, with power, the probability that one will be able to carry out one's will in spite of resistance, "regardless of the basis on which this probability rests" (Weber [1947] 1964, 152).[1] Insinuated as well is the idea that the historical allocation of tasks by gender is implicated in this illusion about where power resides. It provides social preconditions that encourage disjuncture between the way life appears to operate and the way things actually occur. In the analysis that follows, I examine the way power and authority functioned at Bay Chapel and Mount Olive. My conclusion about them is that, as in the opening proverb, those in authority do not always rule, and that this disjuncture, where it occurs, is largely attributable to the importance and value of gender.

At Bay Chapel and Mount Olive, the importance and value of being female or male was not monolithic but diverse. A believer's sex was not a biological given but a multivalent symbol whose meaning shifted depending upon the specific congregational context involved. Three different gender patterns were regularly at play in congregational life. They were sexual polarity (which posits that there are two sexes, distinct from and generally unhelpful to each other), sexual dominance (which posits that there are two sexes, and that one—generally the male—is superior to the other), and sexual unity (which posits that there are two sexes, but that the two are equal). This trifold gendering pattern was initially developed by Susan Palmer in her study of women's involvement in new religious movements. Palmer found that NRMs included normative gender patterns in their religious arsenals, but that each movement tended to emphasize one of these three patterns (Palmer 1993). In intriguing contrast to Palmer's NRMs, where diversity in attitudes toward gender was across groups (Palmer 1994), Mount Olive and Bay Chapel displayed this same range of diversity within each group. All three patterns operated at Bay Chapel and Mount Olive, with shifts occurring from one to the other according to the aspect of religious life involved. In intracongregational gendered ministries, sexual polarity prevailed. In overall congregational authority, sexual dominance took precedence. In normative religious values, sexual unity was evident. Further detail will make these shifts more clear.

In the intracongregational groups of Bay Chapel and Mount Olive, gender frequently functioned as a critical symbol that in itself qualified a person for or, disqualified a person from, participation. The women's and men's ministries of Bay Chapel and Mount Olive were, by title, ministries prescribed exclusively by gender difference. In these gendered ministry groups, sexual polarity prevailed. Women and men were treated as unnecessary to and possibly inhibitory of each other's religious development.

Bay Chapel and Mount Olive women were alike in that they considered the sexual polarity inherent in gendered ministries to be biblically grounded, as well as an expression of common sense. As Nicole explained it,

> I believe in Titus it says that the older women should teach the younger women. So, where there are older women in the Lord, I want to learn from them. Plus, I can teach the younger women. It always makes a mess when the men come in. [Q: Why?] Because we are different. They are going to be self-conscious of what they are listening to. We are going to want to know, well, Am I dressed okay? I don't think about these things—I am more relaxed when I am around women. When a male comes in through the door, it is automatic. It is an in-

nate thing that happens to a woman . . . and the same thing
happens with the men. They strut a little bit higher. Their
heads go up. They start looking like roosters.

In overall congregational governance, gender functioned as
a unique symbol that qualified a person for, or disqualified a
person from, participation. Yet here, sexual dominance prevailed. Men were privileged over women. Males retained exclusive access to key authoritative posts such as the pastoral office,
board membership, and eldership.

The third major congregational gender scheme came to the
fore in the area of religious values. Here, gender was not a de-
cisive symbol: equality of gender prevailed. The salvific relationship encouraged by Bay Chapel and Mount Olive was
shaped not by sexual domination or sexual polarity but sexual
unity, an ontological understanding of gender in which "the
body and its gender [is] a superficial layer of false identity ob-
scuring the immortal, asexual spirit" (Palmer 1993, 346).
Soteriologically, women and men were equal. While the shift-
ing values of gender in congregational life gave authoritative
leadership mostly to males, congregational rhetoric presupposed
that the highest religious good of congregational life—the personal relationship with a living deity—was available equally to
women and men. As far as salvation was concerned, the significance of gender was moot.

These shifts in the importance and value of gender in congregational life set off cross-current waves of power and authority between the sexes that made congregational governance
unpredictable. Exploring the sometimes contradictory influences of these three varying gender patterns reveals the way
Mount Olive and Bay Chapel, while overtly governed by men,
actually operate via complex, multiple bargains of gender.

❖ *Enclaves of Women*

With the Calvary movement, there is a hier-
archy of men. There are men pastors, men on
the board. Women take the out skirting. It's
like, you know, if you're going to be a part of
the movement or whatever, you . . . you either
buy into it or you don't. You live with it. You
flow with it. You, you submit to it.
        —Female staffer, Mount Olive

The participation of contemporary women in North American conservative Protestant congregations presents a painful paradox to those committed to egalitarian relations between the sexes. With little exception, conservative Protestant congregations exclude women from the central leadership role of senior pastor.[2] This is not an isolated instance of discrimination against women; it is one element in the larger, comprehensive pattern of enforced sexual categorization and preferential valuing of males that prevails in congregational life. The regnant theological anthropology of such churches supports a categorical distinction between the sexes that privileges males (Young 1990, 46). Organized such that men alone qualify for senior authority positions (pastors), these congregations provide men with advantageous access to congregational symbolic and economic resources. In the process, they provide men with avenues of unreciprocated authority over women (Young 1990, 47). As a result, from hiring patterns to programming structures, conservative Protestant congregations actively support an ecclesial structure that favors men over women.

At Mount Olive, Molly, Pastor Mike's secretary, indicated that this situation did not bother her, because for the most part she did not find it limiting.

> I've been here a long time. I've seen a lot of people come and I've seen a lot of people go. I have seen a lot of shifts and

changes, and so forth. By the very nature of my longevity, I can see how working for Mike and acknowledging the different positions of women in the church has given me a freedom to do my job, to fulfill what I think is a calling for this point of my life in a very full way. I don't feel like I'm not getting anywhere. Is that clear? I feel like Mike has a responsibility. Mike is the pastor of our church. It's his vision, his leading, God guiding him regarding what Mount Olive will do, how they will reach out and so forth. All Calvarys are based on verse by verse, chapter by chapter Bible teaching. So we've got a good solid teaching. Mike surrounds himself with people who help him to accomplish his vision, and I feel like I am one of those people. I don't feel that by my being a woman, I'm limited in any way.

Molly's view was a common position among believing women. Women did not feel that they were banned from meaningful religious work simply because they could not be senior pastors or sit on the congregational board.

There are a lot of places for women in the church. We have a counseling ministry here. Women do counseling. We have our pro-life group. We have our single parents group—single parents who minister to other single parents that have children. We have our adoption agency. We have the women's Bible study leaders and assistant group leaders. We have women counselors who counsel women in the prayer room. All of our pastors' wives at Mount Olive work here, . . . but not a senior pastor.

Elaine's list is doubly informative. It parades an impressive display of involvement opportunities for women, and at the same time communicates how issues of gender dominate congregational activities. In addition to precluding women from holding particular offices, the categorical difference between women and men that ruled overall congregational life also determined who could speak at particular meetings and established the terminology appropriate to describe such public speech.[3] When a woman preaches (gives the main religious message) at a community event, her speech activity is described as "teaching," and attendance at the event is limited to only women. When a man preaches (gives the main religious message) at a community event, his speech activity is designated "preaching," and both women and men can attend, unless the gathering is specifically designated a men's event, when attendance was limited to men only.[4]

Thus the women of Bay Chapel and Mount Olive do not gain authority from nurturing infants. Instead, the reigning patterns disadvantage women—married or single, with or without children—in terms of their access to congregational authority. On the other hand, as in the proverb cited at the beginning of the chapter, these women do derive power from a subrealm detached from public authority, namely, the all-female enclaves. The female enclaves women's ministries create and sustain militate against the sexual-dominance gender pattern of congregational ecclesiology and provide women with a counterfoil to male dominance in congregational life. They accomplish this by being organized around a gender system of sexual polarity in which women and men are deemed spiritually different, with each "useless or obstructive to each other's salvation" (Palmer 1993, 346). Thus, at Mount Olive and Bay Chapel, the categorical distinction between the sexes that men employed in a gender pattern of sexual dominance to justify their reign over congregational life was used by women in a gender pattern of sexual polarity in women's ministries to justify the formation of all-female enclaves. Operating in a system of sexual polarity, the female enclaves women formed gave them a place where they could discount men's dominance of congregational life. The result is that while both Mount Olive and Bay Chapel are authoritatively dominated by men, each congregation also houses ministries authoritatively dominated by women. In the enclaves or social networks of women that subsequently developed, one might quaintly say, women both rock and rule. The enclaves are major social networks, permeating congregational life, in which women are the central actors and men are marginalized. I therefore begin my description of women's power and authority at Mount Olive and Bay Chapel in the place where women's power takes form: in women's ministry programs and the all-female enclaves they support.

Centers of female religious activity, women's ministry programs at Mount Olive and Bay Chapel are within, yet apart from, the congregation as a whole. At both churches, the senior pastor supervises these ministries, as he does all congregational programming; however, they otherwise are not subject to the all-male governing structure.[5] Women's ministries at Mount Olive and Bay Chapel use the congregation's physical facilities but maintain a level of financial independence, although the level of financial independence each achieved varied greatly. At Mount Olive, women support their own child care, pay for their own speakers, and cover the general expenses associated with group maintenance. At Bay Chapel, women draw significantly more upon the congregation's budget for their activities. For instance, the salary of the full-time associate women's pastor comes directly out of congregational funds.[6]

At both, the strong female enclaves that women's ministries help develop mobilize women's social, economic, and spiritual resources for the benefit of women. That female enclaves should develop within these congregations should cause no surprise. Their genesis is in fundamentalism's sacred dividing wall, the bifurcation of human experience by sex that characterizes all three gender patterns present in congregational life.

In the enclaves, the underpinning of women's authority and power is located in the separate, female-led symbolic universe that women construct and manage through the extensive variety of women's ministry programs. As they participate in these events, women teach and learn sacred things from each other and become accustomed to seeing each other as ritual leaders. By this, they bring to life empowering all-female social-symbolic spaces. According to feminist anthropologists, such sites, separate from their homes, are critical to women's development of female consciousness (Lerner 1993, 233). At Bay Chapel and Mount Olive, the enclaves guarantee it, at least to some extent. They are the generative base of the congregational authority and power of women, and it is to them that women turn when they are in need.

At both churches, male leadership of overall congregational life is pervasive. Men are the senior pastors, the board members, and the elders. As a consequence, outlets for female talent and energy in the congregation as a whole are few. Women generally channel their abilities into women's ministry programs, thereby enriching the symbolic universe of women and strengthening the enclave. At women's ministry retreats, women do all the planning, lead all the study sessions, and preside over any ritual observances, including, from time to time, communion and even baptism. By so doing, women become skilled at developing spiritual resources and their ever-enhancing talents make women's ministry programs potent centers of women's faith lives.[7]

Though all women's ministry activities necessarily involve women, they do not all equally contribute to women's intra-congregational empowerment. Women's Bible studies—a key activity of women's ministries at Mount Olive and Bay Chapel—are highly ambiguous in this regard. The way women study the Bible simultaneously advances and undermines their empowerment. Fundamentalist-literalist, they use a Scottish commonsense-realism approach: the Bible means what it means and says what it says. Mount Olive and Bay Chapel women on memorize Bible verses and then use an inductive approach, individually and within their women's group, to relate the Bible stories they have learned to their own lives. This process of studying the Bible without "exercise of intellectual authority" (Bendroth 1994, 86) results in a curious mixture of empowerment and disempowerment for female believers. Women are empowered because they embrace the Bible as something accessible to them and not as a text understood by an erudite few and intelligible only if a pastor explains it. My interviewees assumed the Bible was a (sacred) book they could read and speak about with as much authority as anyone else. Since all believers are bound by the Bible, and the Bible is a book that can be understood with common sense, then anyone with common sense can interpret it and know what the rules for Christian life together are. Thus women's hermeneutical approach to biblical texts empower them by giving them an accessible absolute from which to negotiate with others in their families and congregations. Given their belief that the biblical text is supreme, the guiding idea (if not always the concrete reality) is that the text is authoritative, not the interpreter; therefore, women contend that they as well as men can read, understand, and draw on its precepts to guide behavior or give advice to others. As the most prominent Bible teacher, the congregation's senior pastor possesses an edge in the interpretive scheme, but only an edge. To fundamentalists, it is the Bible, not the pastor, who mediates between the self and the divine.

At the same time, the inductive approach women employ is disempowering to them. Most importantly, it cuts female believers off from recent historical studies, including feminist studies, of biblical texts that disclose the patriarchal social context of these writings (Schussler-Fiorenza 1900). The idealization of the so-called commonsense approach to the Bible that Mount Olive and Bay Chapel women use fosters among them an unreflective stance toward the historicity of the Bible and an absence of critical concern over how the patriarchal patterns that dominated the ancient world and influenced the codification and canonization of this sacred book now structurally work against them as women.

Overall, the special ministry programs for women that women at Mount Olive and Bay Chapel organize and run give fundamentalist women the opportunity to be highly involved in a symbolic universe of faith managed by women while remaining linked to the congregation's traditional symbolic structure. The result for my interviewees was a profile of religious duality. Through involvement with overall congregational life, believing women acquiesce to a male-dominated religious world; but, in turn, they undercut their acquiescence by establishing and supporting intracongregational female enclaves through their participation in women's ministries. Willing neither to walk away from the religious goods nestled within a patriarchal schema nor overthrow its patriarchal leadership, the Bay Chapel and Mount Olive women I interviewed bargain with patriarchy to get what they want (Kandiyoti 1988, 274).

Obviously, the bargains fundamentalist women strike are far from ideal when viewed from the stance of contemporary egalitarian politics; yet that fundamentalist women do bargain for what they want is more than they typically are given credit for. To be appreciated, these bargains must be considered in the context not only of ecclesial policy but also of the relationship-based faith of believers' comprehensive worldviews. The women of Bay Chapel and Mount Olive are committed to values they interpret as being at great odds with modern culture. Because of this, most female believers find they have more in common with male believers than with any nonbeliever, male or female. To have any chance of realizing their religious goals, they must work with male believers, not against them. Pre-millennialism comes into play here as well: a majority of those involved with Bay Chapel and Mount Olive expect Jesus to return in their lifetimes. For those prone to consider these gender bargains unfair, consider that to the women making them their inherent transitoriness defuses rebellious impulses and provides scant motivation for complaint.

Women and Congregational Authority: Achieved

The enclaves are not the only places where women's authority or power develop in congregational life. Though conservative Protestant congregations are often described as places of monolithic male domination, women normally do occupy positions of authority within them. For some women, this authority is achieved. Women are hired into staff positions based on their skills, knowledge, or training, or the conviction of those doing the hiring that the woman in question has a "call." Historically, it has been easier for women to obtain authority in extracongregational endeavors such as overseas mission work (Bendroth 1990; Beaver 1968). Female missionaries left the harbor of congregational life to teach and testify at sites around the world starting in the 1800s, largely due to the fact that organized women's societies raised the funds to support their efforts (Beaver 1968). The missionary sending agencies, almost exclusively run by men (Bendroth 1990, 89), were not initially enthusiastic about women's involvement in the arena but most gradually deferred to the skill, dedication, persistence, and economic power women committed to mission work (Beaver 1968).

At a Mount Olive service, Mike requested that those preparing to leave on mission activities join him on the platform so the congregation could pray for them. Three men and four women went up, all in their early twenties. Three of the women and all the men were going to minister to prison inmates in the Midwest. The remaining woman, a missionary from Guatemala, was leaving to work at an orphanage in Mexico. During this study, Bay Chapel sent a team of women to Russia for three weeks to minister in prison camps. Several Mount Olive women had been on mission trips to Egypt, Russia, and other sites. The enclaves provided human resources for these journeys and helped financially support them as well.

Women can hold positions of achieved authority in congregational life as well. At Bay Chapel, Ellen was the associate pastor on staff who directed the women's ministry programs. She was hired as an associate pastor after years of experience with women's ministry. Thus, her authority is achieved. Ellen was selected women's pastor by her predecessor and the congregation's senior pastor; however, the story she tells about the day she was offered the post indicates that she understands her work in women's ministry as an independently legitimated spiritual call from God and her selection for the post as a ratification of that call that came without significant effort on her part.

> When I was interviewed, the senior pastor asked, "Is there anything you want to share with me that would make a difference in me hiring you or not hiring you?" I looked at him and I said, "No. There is nothing I want to share with you, because I want to make sure it is the Holy Spirit. I want to make sure it is God that is talking with you. I don't want to influence you one way or another, so I am not going to say a thing." And he said, "Well, you had your chance." I walked out and I thought, There is no way that this guy is going to hire me. The very next day, Jane [the outgoing women's pastor] called and she said, "It's yours, if you still want it. If you still want it, it's yours."

The high level of participation in Bay Chapel women's programs yielded a sizable overlap in the population pools of the congregation in general and women's ministries participants. As a result, interactions between Rory, the senior pastor, and Ellen, the women's pastor, could be and at times were intricate; therefore, the question of Ellen's power as well as authority is a salient one. To Ellen, it was clear what her ministry entails: "I am over all the females in this church. I am the women's pastor over that area of the church, which means . . . anything that has to do with women and the area of Bible studies, counseling, outreaches, ministries from aerobics to discipleship, those kind of things." Still, when the senior pastor instituted a drive to have the entire congregation at Bay Chapel complete a specific study guide, women's ministries fell into line. For the next several months, women used the guide Rory recommended as their primary study material. Though this was the only time identical study materials were employed in women's and congregational programming during the course of this study, the event was notable. It called into question the amount of autocephaly or self-rule in the female enclaves. Though Ellen possessed the title of woman's pastor, the incident hinted that she, at least on occasion, might be functioning as an authoritative follower of male leadership rather than a genuine leader of women.

Intriguingly, this possibility was considered and dismissed by Ellen's loyal subleaders. Queried about the use of the pastor's recommended study guide in women's groups, they told a variety of stories to explain it; however, each indicated that Ellen, independent of Rory, had decided to use the study. "She reviewed the guide, and agreed with Rory that it was highly valuable," Kay claimed.

A number of things remain unknown in any research project. An accurate reading of the political currents and power dynamics of this incident eluded me. I was not able to discover the extent to which the subleaders' stories accurately depicted the events leading up to the women's groups acceding to Rory's recommendation. The only piece of concrete evidence I did collect was the striking similarity in the women's accounts of it. Every woman queried about the materials described their use in the women's groups as a voluntary, independent choice made by Ellen. Thus, at a minimum, the independence of women's ministries at Bay Chapel (understood by participants as under the direction of God) is a value women publicly work to sustain; therefore, it must be acknowledged that at a minimum a potential for autocephaly exists. To the extent that subleaders' stories align with intragroup events, a measure of autocephaly is truly present.

The history of women's achieved leadership at Bay Chapel in programs other than women's ministries is uneven. Women have had and lost and regained the ability to lead minichurches (in-home prayer groups that meet once a week). Nancy attributes these changes to switches in senior pastors.

> At Bay Chapel, some of the stances that they've had in my tenure here are very ironic to me, seeing that the Foursquare church was started by a woman. They didn't want to have women in positions of leadership like a minichurch shepherd. I thought, Well, that's pretty weird. Pretty ironic. But it's not like it really set against the grain with me very much. It was just kind of like, fine. There's plenty of other stuff to do in the kingdom. I don't need to be a minichurch shepherd.
>
> They've backed off from that. I was a minichurch shepherd for a year. It changed because our former pastor, Steve, really felt in examining scripture that women were supposed to be in a subordinate position. Rory clarified it. They were trying to get away from the possibility of having a woman dictating to the head pastor what to do.
>
> There's still a significant number of guys—just regular guys, not in leadership—who don't like the idea of submitting to a woman. It comes up in minichurch if you talk to the minichurch shepherds. To one extent or another, it can be an issue. I had female friends who really went through the meat grinder with that, with people in their minichurches saying, "I disagree" [with female leaders] and they wouldn't leave. They would stay.

Nancy's stories about women's leadership at Bay Chapel reveal how gender biases in the structure of authority as well as in social habits can impede women's ability to attain of achieved authority. The amount of achieved authority available for women remains vulnerable to the vagaries of individual senior pastors. Further, women can gain positions of achieved authority only to discover that some among those expected to acknowledge her authority refuse to do so.

A keynote speaker at a Bay Chapel women's luncheon told those present a story about what happened to her at a mixed-sex meeting where she was invited to speak. During her talk, she had mentioned that she had an ongoing fight with depression and that depression was a family tendency. Afterward, "a man got up and fixed my speech," telling those present that she hadn't meant what she had said. The speaker insisted to the women that she had meant what she said. "Christians do get depressed," she insisted, "just like some Christians are Democrats." Working publicly to shatter the appearance of unanimity in congregational life, the speaker denied that all believers thought alike on holiness, conservatism, or submission. In response, the women broke into loud applause. Still, the speaker proposed no action to address or counteract the suppression of her voice by a male authority—or the customary structural differences of authority between women and men that permitted it to happen—and no one in the audience spoke out to offer one. In this instance, the enclave was an ambiguous locale for women. It provided a place where one woman's story of how her ideas were diminished in a mixed-sex congregational activity by a male authority figure was aired; but it also revealed women's lack of creative alternatives to address the situation, possibly calling more attention to the power of the organizational rules and habits blocking its resolution than to the problem itself.

⬚ *Women and Congregational Authority: Ascribed*

Women also can attain positions of authority within the congregation based on relationships to authoritative men. Here, their authority is not achieved but ascribed. In congregational life, the role of pastor's wife is the most notable such ascribed post. A woman married to a pastor is accorded authority within the group based on her marital link to the male leader. Upon marriage, she becomes, in congregational parlance, a "pastor's wife." Since senior pastors are traditionally male and heterosexuality is theologically mandated, "pastor's wife" is a post necessarily reserved for women; however, it's link to a marital tie has resulted in it often being belittled in analysis, along the lines of Ackerman's comment that it is "an unbearably contradictory role" (Ackerman 1985, 79). Bendroth describes pastors' wives historically as informal leaders with "many responsibilities but little power" (Bendroth 1994, 78). My research at Bay Chapel and Mount Olive indicated that this is not necessarily the case.

At Mount Olive, pastor's wife is the highest position of authority available to a woman. As long as she is married to Mike, Mount Olive's senior pastor, Elaine automatically occupies the authoritative position known as "pastor's wife." At Mount Olive, it is not mandatory that the senior pastor's wife head women's ministries. Elaine does so primarily due to the insistence of congregational women. Notoriously shy, she avoided congregational leadership for years; but the women of the congregation wanted her to lead them, and eventually they got their way. Elaine now heads a women's board staffed by pastors' wives and other leading congregational women. She draws a salary and runs the ministries out of a separate building on the church site, where she has a large, comfortable corner office.

The autocephaly Elaine exercises as head of women's ministries can appear questionable, given her marital tie to Mike; yet in interviews, Elaine, who came to her authority through ascriptive means, described herself in independent, powerful terms. The intramovement norms that condone marriage provide a pastor's wife with nearly unassailable authority. Elaine stated, "I am not a feminist the way the world would view a feminist, but I think some of my views as a pastor's wife and how I personally believe are really feminist. I have strong feelings that I differ with Mike on and he leaves me alone. He doesn't try to convince me. I wouldn't agree with everything he teaches. I don't agree with everything he says. I have strong opinions about how I feel about life. My worldview differs from Mike's." At Mount Olive, Elaine, through the ascribed role of senior pastor's wife, is now a vital component of women's authority as well as women's power.[8]

Women and Congregational Power

As the cases of Elaine and Ellen reveal, the congregational authority women possess at Mount Olive and Bay Chapel respectively is not insignificant; yet, at each church, it is severely limited in ways male authority is not. Given that women make up roughly half of all participants, the question then is, Is women's lack of authority counterbalanced by their access to congregational power? Can women in the nexus of congregational life at Bay Chapel or Mount Olive carry out their wills in spite of the situation of circumscribed access to authority? Do women make up for their relative lack of authority by having more power than men?

Since congregational involvement at Mount Olive and Bay Chapel is voluntary, and since both congregations depend upon the time and money donations of volunteers to survive, it would seem reasonable to assume that even when women are shut out of congregational authority they still possess extraordinary power. To consider the extent to which this is so, I want to focus on the events set off by the sexual misconduct of one of Mount Olive's pastors. These events revealed that congregational women not only had power but could exercise it to change a major pattern of congregational life. Yet they did so in a way that left the form of traditional male authority norms intact. The women effectively maneuvered within the bifurcated realms of meaning their community supports, and drew upon the symbolic resources available there to influence the structures and practices of congregational life. Thus a crisis affecting the morale of the congregation lifted the curtain on what might be best described as a delicate dance between male authority and female power in church life. It disclosed a stark contrast to the monochromatic picture of fundamentalist congregations as places where those who join "submit themselves to the authority of a pastor" (Ammerman [1987] 1988, 56). When trouble hit Mount Olive, the women revealed that they had bargained with, rather than surrendered to, patriarchy. They remained tangible factors in the social control mechanisms of the group.

The crisis began with Mount Olive's all-male pastoral staff. The major duties assigned to this staff include organizing and conducting five weekly congregation services, performing baptisms and marriages, presiding at funerals, overseeing the home fellowship network, and counseling. It was in the process of carrying out this last duty that Larry, a member of the pastoral staff, got into trouble.

While counseling a woman at the church, Larry allowed the interactions between the two to move from a counseling relationship to friendship, and then from friendship to sexual intimacy. Larry spoke openly about the experience.

> When this other person became a friend, the things that I wouldn't share at home, I'd share with her. That became very unhealthy very quickly. All through my whole life, I've been able to handle things. I believe God has gifted me with that gift of administration. But that same thing of being able to

handle a lot of things, turned against—I used it against myself. "This is a friendship. I can handle it," [I said to myself]. And for [a] couple of months, nothing ever happened. You know: nothing physical had happened. But the Scripture also says, "Take heed. If you think you're going to sin, you're going to fall." And I fell. Sexual sin occurred. Intercourse never occurred with her, but *sin*—to disqualify myself from ministry—happened.

My wife, Julie, suspected something and confronted me. So I confessed it to her. Once I told my wife, it was . . . she couldn't . . . she had no one to bounce it off of. So she talked to a friend. [Subsequently] the friend called me [and said], "I can't believe what she is saying about you." I said, "It's true. I have to confess to you that it's true."

So the handwriting was on the wall. This was like three days after [I had told my wife]. I was still working here. [I said to myself], "I don't want Mike [the senior pastor] finding out through rumor or through gossip. I'll tell him myself." So I went and confessed it to him. And I really—I admire [him]. The way he handles pressure. The way he handles crisis. No knee jerk reaction. No anger. [He said,] "Let's pray and see what the Lord wants us to do here." So over the next couple of weeks, as he's seeking the Lord, another rumor would pop up. And one over here. And . . . more rumors. [One day, Mike said to me], "This is getting out of control. Satan is having a field day, and we need to defeat Satan. We need to deflate *him*. This is the first step in that: you need to confess it to the body. It will defuse the rumors, defuse the gossip, and it will start you on the road of restoration between you and your wife, and you and God."

At a well-attended Wednesday evening communion service, Larry made a (nonvoluntary) excruciating public confession. He then left congregational employment and went to work in construction, but he, Julie, and their two children continued to worship at Mount Olive. As a pastor's wife, Julie automatically qualified for the women's ministries board; but, with Larry's termination, her qualifications were gone. Yet the women's board asked Julie to remain a member, and Julie accepted the offer. Julie also continued to oversee the home schooling program of Mount Olive's elementary school. A year later, Mike asked Larry to rejoin the congregational staff. Reconciled and repentant, Larry thought the situation was settled and came back on the staff.

Through this period, a number of women in the congregation remained unhappy. They did not consider Larry's behavior an isolated instance of pastoral adultery. Instead, they attributed it to faulty institutional policy. Men, women concurred among themselves, should not counsel women. "They simply don't understand us," one woman insisted. By taking this stance, congregational women were insisting that the sexual-polarity model that undergirds the enclaves and provides the rationale for women's authority be extended to counseling situations as well. In women's enclave meetings and in casual social gatherings of women, they repeatedly voiced concerns about appropriate counseling policy. At enclave events, Julie was transformed into an idealized symbol of the wronged wife. The phrase "Julie-and-her-troubles" became a trope employed by women to discuss any aspect of the event. In women's groups, leaders who wanted to make a point about women's ability to endure, their fidelity in marriage, or their unique capacity to understand other women would utter the phrase "Julie-and-her-troubles" and heads would nod. At the annual spirituality retreat, women leaders asked Julie to play a prominent role in the women's drama, that of a sexually desirable woman whose beauty kept her from paying attention to God.

As Julie-and-her-troubles developed into a recurrent theme of enclave events, pastors' wives and the women's ministries board began a series of actions, some overt and some ambiguous, to address the women's concerns. At women's meetings, the pastors' wives openly began to teach that women should not go to male pastors for counseling. "Don't throw your jewels [before them]," Elaine taught at one gathering. She told the women that the male pastors had serious shortcomings and that many struggled with their marriages. More ambiguously, the pastors' wives and other women of the church began an informal campaign of conversation within the congregation about counseling procedures.

It didn't take long for Mike to recognize the way congregational winds were blowing. He soon announced that he had decided the congregation should change its approach to counseling. From now on, only women would counsel women. By this act, and in a manner similar to the way he had responded to the congregational pressure to discipline Larry in the first place, he kept the authority of the pastorate sacrosanct: he was the one who made the decision. Yet it was the women who were exultant: their stance of sexual polarity had been affirmed. Pastors' wives and several leading laywomen immediately volunteered to be counselors. They enrolled in special training classes and quickly assumed their new role. Although Mike was officially credited with deciding what the congregation would do, the women's widespread discontent, focused in the enclaves, was the key motivating force behind this substantial alteration of the patterns of Mount Olive's congregational life.

From a feminist perspective, it is important that power exercised by women in such ways be acknowledged in order to disrupt the myth of absolute male rule. Yet, the procedural change effected by the women of Mount Olive was, at best, an ambiguous achievement. The women got the change they wanted, but the public image of the senior pastor's power remained intact. By being flexible, Mike maintained the tradition of male domination. Because men monopolized congregational authority, women had to focus their attention and energies on a single issue to effect change. Since their access to congregational leadership remains structurally limited, women will face the same organizational struggle in the future if and when they want to alter the patterns of congregational life.

Personal Life

While I have so far considered power and authority in terms of intracongregational relations, there are other ways power and authority can manifest themselves through groups. One is intrapsychically, such as in how participation in the group influences the power an individual is able to wield in her or his personal relationships. Ascertaining the extent to which women are being empowered or disempowered in this way by their congregational involvement is a further necessary component of evaluating their power. To do this, I begin by considering the religious ideas women encounter in their congregations.

The highest religious value acknowledged by people who attend Bay Chapel and Mount Olive is the individual's relationship with Christ. Believers describe this by saying that what they are involved in is "not a religion but a relationship" (see chapter 4 for a detailed exploration of this concept). The soteriology implicit in this slogan hinges upon a personal, direct connection with the divine and consequently yields a low-church theology. Although Bay Chapel and Mount Olive women may be active churchgoers, they do not consider church attendance necessary for salvation. The essential soteriological ingredient is an experiential relationship with Christ, cultivated by Bible study.

Julie was a self-described "lukewarm Christian" before she got involved with Bay Chapel. Now her life is different, but she does not consider Bay Chapel or its pastoral staff pivotal elements in this change. It is her relationship with Christ that made the difference. "Religion is what messes up religions. They bring their own doctrine that isn't in the Bible. If you don't see it in the Bible, then where does it come from? It's made up in the religion itself . . . and that has to do with, uh, Pentecostals, it has to do with Presbyterians, Baptists. My [former] religion stopped me from learning the truth, because it was religious."

Julie's ambivalence toward religion and its trappings was common among the fundamentalist women I interviewed, and her widely shared understanding of faith has important implications for fundamentalist women's congregational power. To fundamentalist women, salvation is not mediated by religion (which includes religious institutions and the rituals they offer) but by and through a personal relationship with Christ. This establishes a norm that limits the import and power women should concede to any other aspect of their religious life, including a pastor, who, this key theological precept indicates, is not a necessary mediator. Thus, it is a theological idea that can and at times does militate against the sexist impact on female fundamentalists of male domination of the pastorate.

The soteriological ideas that undergird Julie's attitudes toward religion—that the key salvific experience is open to both women and men, and that church attendance is not mandatory for this experience to occur—are not exclusively held by women, but common among Christian fundamentalists in general. One important implication of these two beliefs is that the salvific ideal of Christian fundamentalists can be interpreted in a surprisingly egalitarian way. To fundamentalists, the approved route to sustain and improve one's relationship with Christ is through biblical study, not through participation in any ritual or rite. This is why Bible study dominates the programming at fundamentalist congregations. Fundamentalists strive to improve their knowledge of the Bible because it is that and that alone which, they believe, brings them closer to God, that which will yield their salvation. And for fundamentalists, anyone can engage in Bible study. Gender is not a bar.

The discord between a congregational ecclesiology that favors men and a soteriology that does not yields an incongruous result. While women can be impeded by the gender pattern of male dominance that saturates ecclesial life—however offset it may be by the symbolic strength and support gender polarity yields in the female enclaves—women still can access the highest symbolic goods available under fundamentalism's sacred canopy. They can and do understand themselves as having a fully engaged and engaging relationship with Christ.

Women's Political Empowerment

Group-derived individual empowerment also can manifest itself politically, that is, in the way it apportions out among its members the ability to deal with other institutions, as well as to direct public attention on behalf of the group toward issues that concern them. At Bay Chapel and Mount Olive, the amount of political empowerment women receive within the congregation changes depending upon the level of analysis involved. At the congregation level, the (male) senior pastor is more politically empowered than anyone else; he speaks for the congregation in its relationship with the community and the state. However, his empowerment is not absolute. He is accountable to the (all-male) board, although its members are people he himself selected. More stringently, his empowerment is limited within the narrow scope of the movement's tradition of biblical rationalism. At the enclave level of analysis, women are more politically empowered than men. Within the enclaves, women conduct cross-congregational retreats and hold regional studies that address the life issues of women. But at the societal level, this empowerment vanishes. Bay Chapel women do describe themselves as considerably more politically aware and involved since joining their congregation. Most attribute this change to Rory, who encourages adherents to be politically involved as a Christian duty. By contrast, Mount Olive women attribute no significant change in the level of political empowerment they experience to their faith. Yet, at both Mount Olive and Bay Chapel, women reported almost no interest in political activism and failed to participate even in the few rallies around women's political issues held at their congregations during this study.

Two sociologists who have analyzed the link between women's congregational involvement and their political mobilization, Robert Wuthnow and Martin Reiserbrodt, offer somewhat contrasting assessments of fundamentalist women's political empowerment (Rieserbrodt 1993; Wuthnow 1990). In his concise analysis of the link, Wuthnow states that his empirical evidence "points toward religion as facilitator rather than as inhibitor" of political involvement by women (Wuthnow 1990, 318). Further, "evidence indicates that conservative women are more likely to manifest a positive relationship between religious involvement and political involvement than are liberal women" (Wuthnow 1990, 319). To Rieserbrodt, it is an oxymoron to describe the activism of fundamentalist women as their political mobilization. From a modern, Western point of view, authority and power women garner within fundamentalism is, he argues, more accurately described as paradoxical than as mobilizing. As in the anti-ERA drive, fundamentalists offer women institutional support to lobby on behalf of their own oppression (Rieserbrodt 1993).[9] Yet, at Bay Chapel and Mount Olive, women proved reluctant political actors, thus contradicting both theories. During my fieldwork, I witnessed the failure of repeated attempts by congregational leaders to politically mobilize them.

▨ *Congregational Anchors of Authority*

*Let a woman learn in silence, with all submis-
siveness. I permit no woman to teach or have
authority over men; she is to keep silent.*
                                    —1 Timothy 2:11–12

To gain some perspective on the value of women's accomplish-
ments in their congregations, the authority and power of women
at Bay Chapel and Mount Olive must be set against the biblical and theological interpretive schemes that prevail in the congregations. According to standard fundamentalist rhetoric, the
norm for authority in congregational life is "male headship."
Fundamentalist pastors argue for it in three steps: (1) they identify the Bible as the sole source of authority, (2) they claim the
Bible is inerrant, and (3) they point to biblical verses which,
they claim, dictate that congregations should be led solely by
men (Marsden 1991, 27). Congregations such as Mount Olive
and Bay Chapel appear to offer a straightforward instance of
institutionalized male domination. This theological stance neither idealizes nor rejects pastoral authority. Pastors are prayed
for under the assumption that an omnipotent, omniscient God
does everything possible to guide their actions. Bay Chapel and
Mount Olive both operate within this understanding of congregational authority, although, as the sections on women's
achieved and ascribed authority reveal, the way this model is
followed varies.

Though males are pastors, the task of preaching "does not
belong uniquely to the ordained ministry; on the contrary, it
can be done and must be done by every believer" (Barr 1977,
31). The pastor is simply someone whose special task is to teach
the Bible, often for scant economic reward. The members of
Bay Chapel and Mount Olive interpret their pastors' "scriptural
mandate" as something that limits as well as grounds pastoral

authority (Weber [1947] 1964, 341). The Bible-studying laity frequently know biblical passages as well as their pastoral leaders do and exhibit behavior indicating that they are quite capable of holding their own against them.

At Mount Olive, there is a long-standing intracongregational joke about the senior pastor's preference for the King James Version of the Bible. Congregants, who generally prefer the New International Version or the New American Standard, consistently manage to ignore his blandishments, wheedling, role modeling, and straightforward requests to change. One night, the pastor's frustration with the situation surfaced in worship. When the time came for him to announce the biblical passages, he told the congregation, "We are going to read this morning from the King James Version. Last week, it sounded like people were speaking in tongues with all the different versions you read from. Do try to get a small, paperback King James and bring it with you. It's amazing when it's all read in King James. I'm the diehard. I know all those other versions are good, but please put up with me. Let's all use the *authorized* version." In response, the congregation laughed—loudly. Next week, they continued to read from their NIVs and NASs.

Still, by retaining exclusive rights to the senior pastorate, males dominate the public speaking time of the gathered community. By so doing, they not only gain a disproportionate amount of ecclesial authority but also (intentionally or inadvertently) introduce symbolic obstacles to women's ability to draw upon the congregation's central good through a tendency to draw illustrative stories from the range of life experiences encouraged by male socialization processes rather than female ones. This makes it easier for males rather than females to strengthen their access to congregational symbolic goods merely by participating in gathered community rituals.

Another critical aspect of males' exclusive possession of the pastorate comes in the male pastors' correlative ability to produce authoritative ideology and influence extracongregational images of the religious movement to which they are attached. Because male pastors are recognized and responded to as the authoritative leaders of these groups, their ideas, acts, and experiences are, more than others, readily translated into concrete artifacts such as books and audiotapes, while the ideas, acts, and experiences of women (and nonpastoral men) rarely become known outside congregational life. Since research into conservative Protestantism tends to rely upon concrete artifacts like sermons as primary source materials, male pastors end up not only dominating the public image of their religious tradition but occupying a disproportionate role in the academic analysis of it as well.

❈ *Summary and Conclusions*

As the refrain cited at the start of this chapter—"The hand that rocks the cradle rules the world"—disrupts typical expectations about who is in charge, at Mount Olive and Bay Chapel power and authority operate in ways that disrupt any absolute link between them. Though Bay Chapel and Mount Olive are biblical-literalist congregations, authority at each is bestowed upon women as well as men, on the laity as well as the pastorate (albeit in disproportionate ratios), while power to alter congregational life can be found outside as well as within official positions of authority. Accordingly, women and men possess some ability to affect congregational life, albeit men more than women, and certain men (i.e., pastors) substantially more than men in general.

While Christian fundamentalism often is portrayed as a seamless movement, particular historical antecedents and surrounding regional factors can markedly influence the way a congregation appropriates fundamentalist ideas and practices (Marty and Appleby 1991). Mount Olive's roots in the Jesus

Movement of the 60s and geographic location in a dense, urban southern California environment are formative elements of its religious life not shared by all fundamentalist congregations. Bay Chapel's oceanside location and connection to a Pentecostal denomination also give its religious life a unique context. The extent to which these and other individual characteristics of the congregations I studied account for the authority and power patterns I encountered within them remains at the level of conjecture; however, every fundamentalist congregation has individual characteristics that shape and influence its ideas and practices. Thus the two are like all fundamentalist congregations in that their religious identity is a continual negotiation between goals and context, with the boundary between the two not always very clear.

The differences between women's roles and women's power at Mount Olive and Bay Chapel hint that even in highly conservative religious movements, diverse responses to gender occur. At Mount Olive, most (though not all) women considered its gender-biased price of admission—unequal access to official congregational authority—as belonging to a set of values irrelevant to them. Capable of brandishing significant power, the predominantly working-class women of Mount expressed scant interest in authority or its trappings. When they wished to influence congregational life, they drew upon the female social networks they had forged and carefully maintained to wield notable intracongregational power, albeit with varying success. The predominantly middle-class Bay Chapel women expressed much more desire for authoritative leadership, and perhaps not inconsequentially also possess some access to institutional authority as well as power. In sum, the women of Bay Chapel and Mount Olive, despite their subordinate status, are powerful congregational actors, though none would state this boldly. The power of women is an invisible organizational principle, uncommented upon but allowed for in everyday life and work.

The cause for this pervasive silence may be survival. Augmenting the sacred gender partition that favors male leadership, there are female and male believers in each congregation who firmly believe that men should be in charge. For women to claim that they exercise power in either congregation would issue a dangerous challenge to a cardinal organizational norm; ergo, fundamentalist women's power may be hidden from pastors, congregations, and even academic researchers to help preserve it. Had I not been present and deeply immersed in Mount Olive's congregational life when the events set off by Larry's adultery took place, I doubt that I would ever have learned what I observed firsthand regarding the role women played in an important congregational change. Given the prevailing norms of male authority that permeate the Christian fundamentalist movement, it is practically impossible for stories about women's power to become part of a fundamentalist congregation's public history. Given the lack of unanimity among women regarding normative gender roles, it is difficult for such stories to survive even as gossip. Instead they sink like stones out of the claimed visible memory of congregational life. Yet they do not vanish. For the future of women in fundamentalism, it is important to note that they can reemerge when currents shift or when the right questions are asked at the right time, making it possible for a new faith history to be born.

My conclusion about the authority and power of women at Bay Chapel and Mount Olive parallels an observation Evelyn Brooks Higginbotham made about the intracongregational dynamics of the black church in the United States. She noted that in spite of the sizable public attention paid to male leaders, the black church is "not the exclusive product of a male ministry but . . . the product and process of male and female interaction" (Higginbotham 1993, 2). While Mount Olive and Bay Chapel differ from the black church in substantive ways, including social history, sociological significance, participant composition, and tradition of the pastoral role, they are alike in that the preaching and writing of male senior pastors in both receives sizable public attention outside congregational life, almost to the exclusion of all other participants.

The believing women of Bay Chapel and Mount Olive are in a double bind as the marginalized of the marginalized. In their stands against reigning cultural values, they experience cultural dislocation with their men; yet, in their religious congregations, they are simultaneously dislocated by their men. At these churches, a united congregational life is only possible because women and men work together to achieve shared religious goals, even as some women work apart to differentiate their interests from men and subsequently press for and achieve change. While this does not imply that women rule the worlds of Bay Chapel and Mount Olive, it does mean that they are not merely passive followers of male pastors. At both churches, women are actively at work shaping congregational life.

The multiple valuations of sex that the diverse gender patterns at Bay Chapel and Mount Olive allocate have much in common with many nonreligious American institutions. Amid public rhetoric of sexual equality, men dominate authority in American institutions from government to banking, from schools to religious congregations. Within these institutions, women frequently respond to gender inequality by doing what the women of Mount Olive and Bay Chapel have done: forming separatist advocacy groups that operate as a counterfoil to men's authority. The critical difference between such secular women's advocacy groups and Christian fundamentalist women's enclaves is in the approach each employs to enhance women's strength within their institution. Patriarchal structures survive by strategic rather than undeviating applications of authority. This is integral to how they endure as a cornerstone of male control (Lerner 1993). Most secular women's advocacy groups work for structural as well as incremental change.

Fundamentalist women do not. At Bay Chapel and Mount Olive, the enclaves address issues that affect women but leave structural factors that ensure the continuance of male authority and power alone. Consequently, the flexible patriarchal governance at these congregations allows women intermittent victories but also sustains men's ironclad control of congregational life. To the extent that male pastors are pressed by female congregants to address particular issues rather than redistribute authority in a nonsexist manner, pastors are able to maintain an image of being responsive to women's concerns, thereby destabilizing women's impetus toward change and retaining congregational authority as a prerogative of males.

My Beloved Is All-Radiant

CHAPTER 4

Experiences and Ideas of Faith

The women of Bay Chapel and Mount Olive will speak unhesitatingly about their religious experiences and ideas to anyone who expresses even a modicum of serious interest in them, but always with a major caveat. What they are engaged in, each invariably will proclaim, is *not* religion. As Elaine, head of women's ministries at Mount Olive, quietly related over a cup of coffee one day, "Religion is man-made. What we are involved in is not religion but a relationship."[1] In this chapter, I leave open the extent to which fundamentalist women are indeed engaged in the kind of direct divine-human relationship they describe to concentrate instead on how gender determines what they, as women, encounter in congregational life when they attempt to cultivate that relationship. To begin, I present an overview of the religious experiences and beliefs that were recounted to me. Then I sketch out the sociocultural context against which these experiences and ideas developed, a context that ranges from the macrolevel of broad cultural gender dynamics to the microlevel of each congregation's sacred gender wall bisecting group life. In keeping with the congregational focus of my study, I spend some time documenting how a sacred gender wall obstructs women's ability to access congregational faith resources that putatively are available to all. Intriguingly, my field studies disclosed that the female leaders of women's ministry programs utilize an amazing range of strategies to improve women's ability to draw on and be empowered by these resources, most notably by reconstellating them in the rituals and study sessions they develop. Finally, I offer an overarching assessment of the influence of fundamentalist gender norms on the faith development of fundamentalist women and men.

▒ *Some Definitions*

While "religious ideas" is a fairly straightforward concept, a brief definition of "religious experiences" might be helpful for those new to the study of religious life who wish to advance their understanding of this often misunderstood and much maligned aspect of religion. Rodney Stark's definition of a religious experience as an encounter people have "between themselves and some supernatural consciousness" (Stark 1965) is the explanation that meshes best with my interviewees' narratives. The religious experiences women recounted were personal, individual encounters with something they perceived to be wholly other than themselves. In keeping with a women's-standpoint approach, I treated the women I interviewed as authoritative sources for whether an experience they had was religious.[2] The portrait of women's religious experiences that resulted from this approach disclosed how most of Mount Olive and Bay Chapel women's religious experiences occur well beyond the boundaries of congregational life. In fact, as I discuss later in this chapter, the congregation was revealed to be the least conducive site for women's religious encounters. These findings indicate that gender is a critical issue not simply in how religious experiences are expressed—that is, in the language or metaphors women use to describe religious experiences—but in whether they happen at all, and if so, where.

Philosophically, the content of an event that may lead a person to describe it as religious can be either explicitly or implicitly divine. When such an experience has explicit religious content, a person typically turns to the terms and metaphors of her or his religious tradition to describe what happened. Maria, at Bay Chapel, told me that one morning she woke up and "saw Jesus hovering near me." Her reference to Jesus provided clear evidence that the content of her experience was explicitly religious. When an implicit religious experience occurs, the person who has it cannot readily link the content of what happened to a specific religious symbol or person as Maria did, and yet will insist that the event was religious, that it was an unfathomable encounter with the sacred. Rudolf Otto once poetically described implicit religious experiences as an encounter with the numinous, with something "felt as objective and outside the self," which results in the individual having "creature consciousness, the emotion of a creature, submerged and overwhelmed by its own nothingness in contrast to that which is supreme above all creatures" (Otto [1923] 1950, 10). While Mount Olive and Bay Chapel women rarely waxed that poetic, the religious experiences they described to me—explicit and implicit—had the kind of world-reorienting effect Otto describes. They were powerful events that substantialluy transformed women's worldviews.

Religious Experiences

Perhaps not surprisingly, given their involvement in a Christian congregation, the women of Mount Olive and Bay Chapel exhibit an overwhelming tendency to have explicit religious experiences. Yet implicit religious experiences, while rare, are described by those who have them as being of considerable import. Though the sacred canopies that cover Mount Olive and Bay Chapel congregational life provide considerable support for human encounters with the divine, the women who had them typically expressed considerable surprise. This is in spite of the fact that intense religious experiences are common among them. Every individual I interviewed related one or more religious experiences of an extraordinary nature. From visions to prophetic foresight, from physical healing to unexpected knowledge, these experiences thrust women into an experiential realm well beyond the range of normal daily events.

When communicating their religious experiences, the women speak circumspectly. They do not depict these experiences as conferring some kind of honor upon them or signaling that they had pleased or delighted God in some way. Though the experience is regarded as authoritative to the extent that it accords with the woman's biblical worldview, it does not convey spiritual authority upon her. To Mount Olive and Bay Chapel women, religious experiences are mysterious. While not ineffable, they are causally inexplicable. Thus, they are spoken about by women with restraint and reverence and more than a modicum of awe.

The religious experiences recounted to me generally fell into one of four categories: interpretive, quasi-sensory, regenerative, or presentory (each will be defined below). While these four types of religious experience are neither mutually exclusive in any one woman's experience nor exhaustive of all the religious experiences described to me, they do encompass the major forms of religious experience that Bay Chapel and Mount Olive women were having at the time of this research.[3]

Interpretive Experiences

At Mount Olive and Bay Chapel, the most common religious experience that women have is interpretive. In an interpretive religious experience, a woman gains the ability to connect confusing or troubling incidents of her life to the stories and ideas of her faith such that the incidents are perceived as fingerprints of the divine rather than harbingers of chaos. The primary result of an interpretive religious experience is that formerly senseless phenomena become intelligible through being fit into a religious schema. Much as a puzzle piece is most puzzling when viewed alone but makes sense when placed in the right spot, interpretive religious experiences take random, painful, or, at best, meaningless events and reconfigure them into a meaningful whole. The events that women described as triggering interpretive religious experiences ranged from the tragic to the mundane: from the kidnapping and murder of a child to deciding which house to buy. Whatever the situation, the chief benefit of an interpretive religious experience is its ability to unleash energy for action. A woman inspired by an interpretive religious experience feels free to act and does so.

A central characteristic of an interpretive religious event is its attribution by the one who has it to a power outside the self. Though Mount Olive and Bay Chapel women ascribe value to the religious insights they gain from their joint Bible study, they carefully distinguish between insight garnered through study and the transcendent insight that results from interpretive religious experiences, which break into their normal mode of thought. Moreover, the ability to assess this difference accurately is deemed a sign of spiritual maturity.

Like many enclave women, Martha, a Mount Olive adherent, describes her ability to decipher interpretive religious experiences as a skill that has improved over time. Her first interpretive experience occurred shortly after she got involved with enclave ministries. A brother and sister-in-law's lapse of faith bothered her tremendously, but she had done nothing about it. Before her religious commitment, Martha would not have commented on a family member's spiritual state. But now she considers the declining faith commitment of two family members a serious problem; still, she hesitated to get involved. Martha decided to pray for her brother and sister-in-law during her enclave group's closing prayer. As she did so, Martha got what she simply calls a feeling. When this feeling subsided, Martha told the other women present about it. The group immediately discussed the phenomenon and concluded that it was a message from God to Martha prompting her to speak to her brother and sister-in-law about their lapse. Now, years later, Martha can easily decipher such religious feelings when they come and has learned to credit them to a transcendent source. "Back then, [I] just [got] an impression, a feeling. Now, it's really easy for me to discern when the Lord is speaking to me. I used to think to myself, Wow! That's real insightful; you had a real neat idea there. Now I know it's not me. It's the Lord."

Bay Chapel and Mount Olive women posit a direct link between interpretive experiences and enclave activities, something my field observations confirm. Interpretive religious experiences took place at every enclave event I attended (and never in general congregational gatherings). One factor probably contributing to the preponderance of interpretive experiences at enclave events is that at enclave meetings women exhibit considerable interest in such experiences and willingly invest time to assess them. Through this, enclave meetings allow women to validate or deny each other's religious voices and decrease their reliance upon a male pastor's religious insight. In the process, they also provide a female-centered locus for the development of religious experience capital.

Sensory Experiences

A less frequent but more powerful religious experience reported by the Mount Olive and Bay Chapel women is of the quasi-sensory variety. This is a religious experience in which the primary medium is one of the five senses, although the extent to which the senses actually are involved is rarely unambiguous. States of consciousness vary in sensory religious experiences. At Bay Chapel and Mount Olive, women reported having sensory experiences while they dreamed as well as when they were awake.

The few times I was present during sensory religious experiences, they took place during the closing prayer of a cell group; however, women also spoke of having them when alone in their homes. To Nicole at Bay Chapel the sensory religious experiences that her enclave involvement encourages are a natural outgrowth of faith. "It's a connection, a oneness with the Lord. I feel it physiologically. I feel the hair on my arms go up. I feel the hair on my back go up. I feel my heart racing. A peace that is supernatural happens deep inside of me. Sometimes it is in my heart. Sometimes it feels deeper, right in the pit of my stomach. I have felt it even deeper than that. I think the Lord allows me to feel how he feels. It is like a compassion."

While enclave events encourage religious experiences, the religious experiences that enclave women have expand beyond the parameters of enclave events. Nicole's sensory religious experiences began in her own home when, after several months of enclave participation, she decided to push her faith past what she perceived to be its boundary point. She wanted to know, Was it based on anything real? From the striking intimacy of the opening public prayers of enclave meetings, Nicole had determined that no subject was off-limits when it came to prayer. Alone at home one evening, she prayed about her doubts, and the next day, she had her first sensory religious experience.

One night I said, "Lord if you are real, please reveal yourself to me." I went to sleep with that thought on my mind. The next morning, he woke me up early. I never get up early, but I woke up. There was a rainbow outlining the cross in my room. I have woken up morning after morning, year after year, looking at that cross and there was nothing unusual about it. I did not want to move from that spot. I felt as if I was being bathed in warmth right there. The presence of the Lord was so real and precious at that point that I felt as if I was lying in his arms.

As with interpretive experiences, women who have sensory encounters tend to seek communal validation of them in enclave discussion groups. This can and frequently did trigger an increased involvement in enclave activities, which in turn set off an increased frequency of sensory religious experiences. The more women turned to the enclaves to interpret their religious experiences, the more religious experiences they had.

Regenerative Experiences

It is important to note that Bay Chapel and Mount Olive women do not associate all the religious experiences they have with their enclave involvement. Regenerative religious experiences are a good example of this. Regenerative religious experiences occur when the divine/human encounter reenergizes the individual. The regenerative event itself may take a number of forms, but the primary result is that a wandering, confused, possibly destructive personality is empowered to renew her life.

Most women identified regenerative experiences as occurring during their initial religious conversion, when passionate, moving episodes of this kind impelled many toward a transformed life. To Cicely, a thirty-four-year-old Cajun participant in Bay Chapel, empowerment is insufficient to describe how her religious experiences have regenerated her. To Cicely, divine/self encounters have revolutionized her life.

> I don't know where I would be without God. I would probably be loaded on drugs, doing pills, having to go through all the stuff I've gone through before. I could be dead, because of wrong choices made while being under the influence. It's really that serious. I mean, if those were the choices that I'd made instead of having faith. That's the choices I'd made in the past. If things got tough, I'd just check out. No program ever worked for me. But God works for me, and my faith works for me.

In religious studies and sociological discourse, the religious validity of regenerative experiences such as the one that Cicely recounts has been undermined at times by being labeled the "triumph of the therapeutic." Trapped in the distorting glare of such a reductionistic interpretive framework, Cicely's exultant comment that "God works for me" can be categorized as an example of how people harness religious faith to achieve personal, psychological ends in the modern world (Reiff 1966); however, in the enclaves, Christian fundamentalist women overtly work to countercolonize therapeutic language by linking its terms and insights to biblical stories. A Mount Olive cell group leader explained this difference to me one day. She claimed that the cultural currency of members' language is not a sign of their being captured by the culture; rather, it results from their ongoing effort to missionize it.

Presentory Experiences

Presentory religious experiences, while intriguing, were among the most rare that women recounted. At both Mount Olive and Bay Chapel, women's presentory religious experiences occurred almost exclusively when women gathered in large groups over long periods of time, such as during a weekend spirituality retreat. In a presentory religious experience, a woman has a direct, nonsensory experience of something she identifies as God.

Cognition-driven, presentory religious experiences result in a leap in a woman's understanding or acceptance of the divine, and frequently result as well in a woman obtaining knowledge about people or events in ways that cannot be readily explained. At a Mount Olive spirituality retreat, one Bible study leader suddenly *knew* that another female believer who had been married but childless for ten years soon would become pregnant. At a Bay Chapel Saturday luncheon, a women's ministries newcomer suddenly *had* to communicate a specific message she did not understand to a person sitting at the next table whom she did not know. In relating the details of these events, each woman insistently described them as profoundly religious occasions, moments when she felt that her thoughts had become the very thoughts of God.

When Kiersten, at Bay Chapel, strives to explain what her religious experiences are like, her description could qualify as a dictionary definition of a presentory religious experience. "God puts thoughts in your mind. He puts certain ideas. Especially when I need help with a certain situation or issue. Then . . . the way I pray is kind of different. I just pray within myself. I just talk to God . . . and sometimes I get, like, 'Okay. What about this?'" Like the other forms of religious experience, presentory religious experiences are criticized and validated or rejected by an interpretive community of women.

Validating Religious Experiences

As indicated in the discussions above, Bay Chapel and Mount Olive women do not facilely accept an unusual experience, either their own or someone else's, as something that necessarily represents an authentic divine/self encounter. Instead women narrate such experiences if and when they occur to the members of their cell group. The criteria women employ within their cell group to evaluate someone's experience include its compatibility with biblical teaching, as well as whether the aftereffect encourages or discourages actions that reflect the group's comprehension of Christian ethical norms. Religious experiences accepted by a cell group become part of an enclave's stockpile of symbolic goods, a religious resource that provides women with an ongoing record of how the God they worship notices, recognizes, and interacts with them. In this manner, the female enclaves at Bay Chapel and Mount Olive both encourage women to consider an internal religious voice as potentially authoritative and cultivate women's abilities to critically analyze such promptings and accept or reject them.

Place and Religious Experience

The relevance of place for women's religious experiences is considerable. The religious experiences of Mount Olive and Bay Chapel women occurred

- during the worship portion of a regular service (which women regularly help lead)
- while engaged in enclave events (which women always lead), or
- when alone at home (where women direct their own faith activities)

Note that each is a place where women exercise authority as well as power and have significant "official" roles according to their religious worldview. Although women closely correlated faith ideas with congregational sermons, no woman claimed to have had a religious experience during one. Thus, at both Mount Olive and Bay Chapel, the place in congregational life where women possessed the least authoritative presence was also the place least conducive to their experiences of divine presence.[4]

Gender, Religious Experiences, and Congregational Norms

A central point of this chapter is that the religious experiences that the Mount Olive and Bay Chapel enclaves encourage differ from the norms of overall congregational life. In the overall congregational life of both churches, public gatherings are dedicated to teaching the religious ideas that make up the sacred canopy. Senior pastors at each congregation discourage displays of religious experience at public events, because they wish to focus believers' attention on Christian fundamentalist ideas and the biblical grounds for accepting them. Privileging believers' minds over their bodies, the dominant rituals of overall congregational life encourage a mind/body split, but in the female enclaves this hierarchy of ideas over feelings vanishes. Sacred life in the female enclaves of both congregations revolves around a dialectic of religious ideas and experiences, thereby encouraging a mind/body integration.

⬚ Women's Religious Ideas

The authorized meanings of the religious ideas Bay Chapel and Mount Olive make available to women cannot be easily aligned with the use female congregants make of them. Here, again, the enclaves play a cardinal role in fashioning women's faith, for during enclave meetings women with questions about Bible passages and Christian life are readily listened to with respect and answered (in contrast to the regular services, where leading men speak and everyone else is expected to listen). In discussing their understandings of key theological doctrines such as God, the Bible, and faith, women divulge how they wrestled with these traditional Christian concepts to determine what was trustworthy to believe.

God/Jesus/Holy Spirit

An important factor in relationship-based faith is the question of who the personal God is with whom women are attempting to have a relationship. During interviews, women spoke easily and lengthily about their waking and dreaming encounters with God. When asked to describe God, some women refuse, pointing to a scriptural caveat concerning our limited perceptin of the divine: "For now we see through a glass, darkly; but then face to face. Now I know in part; but then shall I know even as also I am known" (1 Corinthians 13:12).

Irene, a thirty-seven-year-old Mexican-American women's leader at Mount Olive, is one who was reluctant to discuss what she thought God was like. She regards the question as unanswerable by any human being. "I wouldn't want to even say. We in our own human minds can envision what we think God looks like, but I don't know." Darla, a thirty-year-old participant in Mount Olive's women's Bible study who attended a Calvary Costa Mesa for regular services, weaves a description of God with rationalist, empirical threads, bound up with her interpretation of biblical precepts.

> We don't know what he looks like; but, if you want, God is a spirit. We don't really know what a spirit looks like. God never says. That's why he came in human form. When I associate myself with God, a lot of the times I think of Jesus, because he was human. But that isn't what God looks like—and we don't know what Jesus looked like. We have no idea. Nobody drew a picture. I'm sure he did that on purpose. I associate God as—a being—whatever you want to call that. If he's a cloud, or whatever, he has the capacity of knowledge, all my

capacities. He created me . . . but much, much more, of course. I don't see him as a physical being.

Elaine, the overall leader of women's ministries at Mount Olive, describes God in concrete physical terms; but, when she extended her descriptive effort, this concrete portrait is undermined by a second, more abstract one.[5]

> I think God is male. I think he is a lot of light and a lot of white. I don't think of him as how he looks. I think of him more in the realm of emotion. I think he is pure love. I think he is faithful. He is just. I am not sure how those things look . . . but I know they have got to be really attractive.

While Elaine was the only woman I interviewed who overtly claimed that God is male, the women invariably used only masculine imagery and metaphors to describe God and only masculine pronouns to refer to God. In response to a query regarding how women would respond if God was referred to in a prayer as "Mother," only one Bay Chapel woman responded favorably, claiming she was "open to it"—not exactly a ringing endorsement.

For Mount Olive and Bay Chapel women, stories from the life of Jesus help make God more accessible to them, more tangible, more real. Yet they view Jesus differently than their senior pastors did. Rory presents Jesus as a norm that believers should live up to. He claims, "Jesus had to live, just like you and I," so that "Where Jesus fulfilled all righteousness, we must fulfill all righteousness."

In contrast, the women of Bay Chapel and Mount Olive describe Jesus using connective metaphors. He is the being who keeps their religious life from becoming "religion." Nicole, at Mount Olive, speaks of this relationship language as a hermeneutical tool that made her connection with Christianity possible. "When he [Pastor Mike] told me about Jesus Christ, that

Jesus was the bridge . . . that Jesus understood, things started working. Before I had wondered, Is there someone who understands?" Mary describes Jesus as a kind of litmus test for one's faith. A woman has to respond to the dramatic events of Jesus' life as detailed in the Bible if she is to be considered truly godly. "What it comes down to is, Are you born again? Did you have that change of mind and change of heart, knowing that what Jesus did on the cross at Calvary changed your life? Did you receive that salvation, that sacrifice?" Janet, at Bay Chapel, emphatically portrays Jesus as the center of her life. "Jesus is everything and everything. Everything revolves around him. I live my life for the Lord. He is my very, very, very first priority." But overall women spoke far less about Jesus than about God, though they referred to the two practically interchangeably. For instance, when discussing the relationship that is the foundational dynamic of their faith lives, women alternated in no discernable pattern between describing it as a relationship with Jesus or with God. To Mount Olive and Bay Chapel women, no firm distinction exists between them.

The Holy Spirit is the third figure women mention in connection with their relationship with God. Amy, an Asian-American member of Bay Chapel, describes the Holy Spirit as profoundly immanent, as a being that dwells within each individual, that gives advice and instruction regarding personal behavior. "The Holy Spirit is someone that lives in you. It is kind of like a conscience. It tells you when you're doing something right or wrong." To Nicole, the Holy Spirit is a force emanating from God that wise believers allow to rule their lives. "He came to give us direction. He came to give us light. Some are homeless because God wants them to minister there. We are supposed to bloom where we are planted, and make the Holy Spirit president of our bodies."

Quite fascinatingly and somewhat at odds with mainstream Christianity, women regularly described the Holy Spirit as an

ontological aspect of being human that congregational teachings help them understand. To them, it is the regulatory principle of God's order lodged within the self.

The Bible

The centrality of the Bible as sacred text in the religious life of
Bay Chapel and Mount Olive is an overwhelming fact. Bible passages are read aloud and expounded at every congregational
gathering. Bible study classes are held throughout the week.
Every day small group Bible studies take place in believers'
homes. The minimal position that women have in the Bible
means that to access any liberatory potential in the text, women
must read against it—a sophisticated hermeneutic difficult for
all but the most disciplined of readers.

None of my interviewees describe this as a problem. They
define themselves using the same phraseology as the members
of the East Coast Southern Baptist congregation studied by
Nancy T. Ammerman. They are, they claim, Bible-believing
Christians (Ammerman [1987] 1988). The Bible is celebrated
by Mount Olive and Bay Chapel women, who claim they are
inspi red by its male and female role models equally. Phrases
women use to describe their serious interest in Bible study include, "I just got hungry," or "I needed to be fed." When I asked
women why they employed such tangible, biological language
to describe what motivated them to join a Bible study group,
women frequently became relatively inarticulate, yet insisted
that for them Bible study with other women is physically and
psychically sustaining.

For Judith, Bay Chapel's multiple services, progressive music, and extensive programming had nothing to do with her decision to get involved with the congregation. She wanted to
learn about the Bible; so when she found a congregation that
emphasized Bible teaching, she stayed. "Religion didn't impress

me. I wanted to hear the truth from the Word of God. When I found that, I accepted that church." Anne's attitudes toward Mount Olive echo Judith's comments. "I never took Rory's word. I went to the Bible. That's the first thing I did, when I began renewing my faith. I started studying the Bible and praying. Going to church and going to Bible studies isn't your faith. I did that, and I fell from the church. I was led astray. So I studied the Bible and studied what they were teaching. Was it truth? I never take anybody's word as truth until I back it up."

Mount Olive and Bay Chapel women do not deem a Bible study group good simply because it addresses the Bible. They evaluate it based upon whether it helps them grow in their relationship with God. This meant that a study group, even though biblically based, could be negatively evaluated by women. To Nancy, a Bible study she attended before she joined Mount Olive was highly detrimental to her. "I always wanted to be in Bible studies in church, because that's where I felt good. I stayed in church until I couldn't take it any more. I tried to commit suicide. There were certain scriptures that stayed in my mind. People . . . preached at me to submit. 'Submit' became a very nasty word to me. I felt really betrayed. . . . I never spoke of Christ or my relationship with Christ for ten years after that." Currently a women's leader at Bay Chapel, Nancy now evaluates how a study group plans to approach the Bible before getting involved with it, rather than jumping blindly into a group merely because the Bible is its focus.

The fact that the women's ministry programs at both congregations center on Bible study is a sign of their modernity. Such intimate learning clusters where women discuss and integrate biblical stories with the stories of their personal lives were unknown a generation ago, when biblical knowledge was culturally assumed rather than actively sought (Brereton 1991, 83). In an attempt to address the spiritual vacuum that marks modern times, fundamentalist women interact with each other to develop dexterity in faith; they hope to attain a level of spiritual, intellectual, and emotional integration they could not find in the wider culture.

Relationship-based Faith

At Bay Chapel and Mount Olive, relationship with God is strengthened through Bible study—something women and men are equally encouraged to do and supported in doing. When it comes to their relational ideal, at Bay Chapel and Mount Olive "there is neither Jew nor Greek, there is neither bond nor free, there is neither male nor female: for ye are all one in Christ Jesus" (Galatians 3:38).

For Nicole, a former Roman Catholic now actively participating in Mount Olive's women's ministries, a connection with the religious goods of Christianity had been impossible until she encountered relationship-based faith. She was as unable to make the connection between what she heard in church and her own life. She observed ritual acts, but the religious goods they putatively represented proved elusive. "In Catholicism, there wasn't a message coming across to me. They took ritual readings from certain biblical passages, but there was no actual bridge work to help people like myself get the message. It was like watching a TV program. They did everything very structurally, without laying out a bridge to us. So I could never come across it."

For Vicky relationship-based faith pulled her closer to God than to anyone else in her life. Though she uses a simile of romantic love to describe her new faith, she qualifies it by claiming that a relationship with God is beyond anything human interrelationships can achieve. "It's emotional for me. It's like being with someone that you are totally, totally in love with and receiving that love back from them. In worship, relationship with the Lord goes far beyond that. It's beyond anything you can experience with a human being. Definitely."

To Judith, a relationship with God is life's central purpose for all humanity. She explains why this is so through an overarching interpretation of the cosmos. "Why did God make life? Why did he make us? Why did he create us? I think we were made for a relationship with him. He made us to show us what life is, and how he enjoys what he's made, no matter how imperfect life is. I know that it will be wonderful and this and that in heaven, but this is where we are now. This is my life that he's given me. A part of this is the beginning of how it will be in heaven."

Judith's comments disclose how a doctrine of God as well as a theological anthropology underpin relationship-based faith. The doctrine of God it assumes has much in common with Paul Tillich's interpretation of the teachings of the early Christian apologist Justin Martyr, who perceived God as a creator God who was "the acting power behind everything that moves" (Tillich 1967, 28). The theological anthropology relationship-based faith assumes is aligned with ancient Christian traditions: the human being is for God. Judith describes herself, along with all humanity, as God-created, and endowed by God with an essential nature that can only be fulfilled in God relationships.

Organized around the possibility or probability of an encounter with a "personal God," Bay Chapel and Mount Olive encourage believers to develop one-on-one relationships with this entity, understood as creator of the universe and savior of humankind. Given the number of near and actual divorces that Bay Chapel and Mount Olive women painfully attest to in their conversion stories (see chapter 2), the metaphor of relationship for one's primary religious experience—putatively, an intelligible, consistent, dependable relationship—may hold a special appeal that increases the probability of conversion among the divorce-prone living in dense urban environments. The precise language of positive relationality, the image of an unbreakable, wholly benign relationship between God and the self, may alleviate the emotional pain engendered by a broken human relationship. Further, the high mobility and sizable rate of connection with strangers inherent in modern life demand that individuals regularly be able to account for themselves to new others. Absence of substantial shared history between people requires that each be able to tell stories about the self that establish the familiarity necessary for relationships to develop. For the divorced or divorcing, a story of a good relationship with God can be used to offset the negative weight of a bad relationship with a spouse or partner.[6]

Female believers judge congregational activities by the two oppositional categories of relationship and religion. Relationship sets the boundaries of their sacral world; religion is outside it. Relationship involves sacred behavior; religion is its profanation. And the touchstone that allows them to distinguish between the two is the Bible.

Mary, a member of the staff at Mount Olive, divulges how the value distinction believers make between relationship and religion diminishes the importance of congregational life. "There are just too many things, too many man-made traditions. They can keep you tied to a religion. In scripture, Jesus said, 'Follow me.' Religion is what yokes people into believing that if they leave a particular church they will lose their salvation. They are damned. If they are fearful of that, what are they holding on to?"

Jane, an active Mount Olive participant who got involved ten years ago when she was in her early thirties, discusses the change relational faith made in the way she understands herself. She describes it in terms of a locus of personal identity. "I was spiritually dead before. Now I'm spiritually alive. God created us to be spirit as well as flesh, and the spirit is truly me.

That's what lives inside [my] earth suit. Before I knew the Lord, that part of me was something I wasn't even really aware of. It was unregenerate. It was not being used. It was just there. I think we all have a realization that there's something there, but we don't quite know what it is. I didn't, until the Word of God brought it to life."

For women who deem the traditional worldview of fundamentalist congregational life acceptable, the personal rewards relationship-based faith bring can be immense. Among the women I interviewed, all but two got involved on their own and subsequently induced their spouses to attend or were trying to do so. Women who were successful in this claimed that after their husbands got involved, their marriages improved.

Manifesting the sacred canopy's norm of exclusively male imagery for the divine, regular congregational services at Bay Chapel and Mount Olive symbolically shortchange female believers, but the female enclaves provide a symbolic world hypercharged with female images (albeit one that revolves around a male salvific deity). This second symbolic world creates critical breaks in congregational norms through which dexterous female believers can maneuver to achieve remarkably individualistic interpretations of their faith.

In the overall congregational life of Mount Olive and Bay Chapel, religious ideas are showcased in the sermons preached at the regular services and are presented by a single male leader. In all-female enclaves, women work out faith conversationally in small groups. In overall congregational life, believers' religious experiences are controlled and discouraged by pastors, except during conversion. In all-female enclaves, women spur each other on to achieve supple relationships to the transcendent, albeit for immanent ends. Using the faith skills they cultivate in enclaves, female believers draw upon their relational connections with and ideas about their God to make decisions about jobs, alter personal habits, face life choices. In overall congregational life, male senior pastors habitually illustrate sermons using personal stories associated with male socialization. The enclaves, in contrast, serve as interpretive communities of and for women, addressing the experiences of female believers that fall outside the customary metaphors of pastoral storytelling. Providing a symbolic alternative to overall congregational life, the female enclaves at Mount Olive and Bay Chapel undermine many of the patriarchal elements of Christian fundamentalism.

At the same time, the enclaves simultaneously support Christian fundamentalist patriarchalism. By luring active women to invest themselves in a congregational subsection, they abet male dominance of overall congregational life. Thus, ironically, the enclaves that are the primary source of women's empowerment in Christian fundamentalist congregations are also a principle source of their disempowerment. Siphoning off the time and energies of some of the most talented congregational women from overall congregational life, they help keep women under the sacred canopy of Christian fundamentalism who might otherwise deem its gender biases unacceptable and either press for change or leave.

Structural Factors of Women's Religious Ideas and Experiences

Within Mount Olive and Bay Chapel, participants encountered religious resources that formed a symbolic world.[7] This world offered an interpretive grid through which adherents could filter thoughts about life events to determine their "true" worth and meaning. In the symbolic universe of the congregation, the Bible anchored intragroup authority. The senior pastor was the leading Bible teacher, and fundamentalist norms of biblical interpretation prevailed (Boone 1989). In the congregational symbolic worlds of Mount Olive and Bay Chapel, men did all of the preaching and most of the leading. Female and male participants alike were encouraged to extricate meanings from this cache of resources to guide their faith lives.

The religious ideas, images, language, metaphors, and stories of this symbolic world prescriptively defined religious experiences. In regular services at Mount Olive and Bay Chapel, male pastors instructed participants that religious experiences must be grounded in and validated by rational encounters with biblical texts. Since rationality is a communal process, experiences had to be communally authenticated before being conceded as religious. Yet men dominated public authority and figured prominently as Bible interpreters. As a result, the symbolic world of the congregation prescriptively placed women's religious experiences publicly and privately under the external or internalized, or most likely both, watchful eyes of male authority figures—persons who, in the prevailing theological anthropology, were defined as essentially different beings. Further, the minimal attention paid to women in the Bible provided women with fewer same-sex textual resources with which to interpret their religious experiences.

The primary place believers were exposed to the resources of the congregational symbolic world was in the mixed-sex Sunday morning weekly congregational worship service. At a Bay Chapel women's Bible study, Ellen referred to them as "regular" services. The label is apt. Bay Chapel and Mount Olive "regular" services are aimed toward committed Christians as well as newcomers. The regular Sunday services draw the largest number of adult believers together and therefore, in a very real sense, regulate congregational religious life. In this regulatory task, the Sunday service prescriptively defines religious ideas and experiences in gender-salient ways.

Regular Sunday services at Bay Chapel and Mount Olive are composed of two segments. The first is called "worship" and is dedicated to congregational singing. The second is referred to as "teaching" or "study." Mostly, it consists of a Bible-based sermon given by a male pastor. According to Mike, this simple structure was becoming increasingly popular with other congregations. "I'm seeing the church coming back to study the Word and loving the Lord. None of this elaborate ritual stuff. Dump it, man. Let's get back to the basics. Worship and study." Each of these segments prescribed women's religious roles as different from men's; however, the prescriptive worldviews each presented, while agreeing about the importance of gender, did not match in the specific significance attached to it.

Worship

Worship is the primary means by which Mount Olive and Bay Chapel ride the wave of cultural change.[8] As opposed to organ-accompanied hymns or choir-performed anthems, Mount Olive and Bay Chapel employ electric guitarists, drummers, and song leaders to unite adherents in choruses marked by abbreviated lyrics and uncomplicated melodic structures comparable to those used in advertising jingles. The choruses are powerful generators of community within congregational life: they are its folk music, its musical voice. Often written by ordinary men and women, choruses tell simple stories about adherents' transforming faith experiences.

As an indicator of the extent to which women's religious experiences are structurally prescribed by congregational influences, worship is intriguing. It constitutes a sizable segment of each regular service and gives women a notable public role to perform. Male pastors lead worship, but women lead the songs. They stand at the front of the church along with the male pastor and at the same distance from the congregatin, leading the singing and modeling worship demeanor. With hands raised and eyes closed, two to three women each week stand on the stage singing, awash in religious ecstasy during worship as if unaware of the crowd's presence. These song leaders have slight ability to direct what they sang; however, their presence communicates. As female believers centrally participating in the largest congregational event, they introduce powerful female images into the symbolic amalgam of congregational life.

The male pastors at Mount Olive discourage charismatic responses in public gatherings. This provides little room for individual deviance in worship. Bay Chapel presents a slightly different situation. Worship there often becomes highly emotional. From the pulpit, the pastors neither encourage nor discourage this charismatic behavior. Absent any sanction, many believers reproduce the religious ecstasy of the female song leaders by singing, clapping, crying, at times exclaiming aloud as the music plays. Some fall to their knees in ecstasy. Others dance in place at their seats. For Nicole, emotional, free worship was a mark of Bay Chapel's authenticity. "I liked the style of worship at Bay Chapel. I liked the people. They didn't seem fake. They seemed sincere in their worship, in their adoration. Nothing seemed mechanical. I liked their openness in accepting me anyway I was. I didn't have to wear my Sunday best. I thought, I know my God would accept me anyway I was. For women, worship's expressivism distinguishes it as a gathering centered on relationship-based faith rather than religion.

Sermons

During the sermons at Mount Olive and Bay Chapel, male pastors lead the show.[9] At Mount Olive, verse-by-verse expositional teaching of the Bible prevails. At Bay Chapel, sermons are Bible-based, but topical sermons, in addition to expositional sermons, are standard fare. The total dominance of the sermon segment by men affected women's religious experiences and ideas in two important ways. First, it presents men as the sole source of intellectual authority at congregational gatherings.[10] On very rare occasions, women are invited by the senior pastor to speak in regular services, but their speech is limited to testimonies. Louise, involved with Mount Olive since she was a teen, explained the difference between the two. "A testimony is about your personal life. You describe what the Lord's done and how he's done it, using it as an encouragement to others. Teaching is, 'Now we are going to study 1 John.'" When a woman testifies in a regular service, she introduces an image of an embodied female believer into the worship milieu, but the image was more constrained than that the pastor provided to male believers. Women are publicly limited to participating in ways that showcase them as beings to whom faith happens. Women can anecdotally speak about faith, but they cannot analyze or discuss biblical texts in a public, mixed-sex regular Sunday service to generalize about what believers should do or become. Men, of course, are presented as people to whom faith happens as well, but they are also allowed to be seen as beings who contribute to the authoritative study of the sacred text of their faith.

In sermons, women's ideas and experiences are marginalized. The stories male pastors draw upon to make Bible passages vivid or accessible are disproportionately drawn from socialization experiences historically associated with men. For example, during the time I attended services at these two churches, no male pastor ever drew upon his experiences with quilting or breast-feeding to illustrate a sermon point (activities historically linked to female socialization and life experience); yet pastors made I heard scores of references to war and football (activities historically linked to male socialization and life experience). In regular worship services, the cognitive goods of sermons conveyed to all are packages of meaning more accessible to male participants.

Religion/Relationship

The religion/relationship opposition is a major component of congregational rhetoric at both churches. Mike teaches adherents that the difference resides in the site of initiative: "Religion is man reaching up and trying to touch God. Relationship is God touching us." At each church relationship is the principal religious metaphor, the North Star of the congregation's symbolic world. Relational experiences with God are the raison d'être of the congregations. While Bay Chapel and Mount Olive as institutions manifest organizational patterns and behavior similar to those of other social institutions, in this they distinguish themselves from most (but not all) nonreligious organizations, which generally claim more finite, limited purposes.

In religious traditions adherents generally do not consider themselves constructors of the sacred. Instead, they understand themselves as being constructed by it (Erickson 1993, 139). By prescribing religious experiences in individualistic terms, Bay Chapel and Mount Olive's emphasis on relationship-based faith enhances this nonreflective proclivity among their attendees. Working within the definitional schema of relationship-based faith, congregational rhetoric lauding relationship does not do away with religion; it simply masks it, making the institutionally structured similarities of the relationships with God that participants developed harder for them to see. Since gender is a significant factor in the institutional aspects of religious life, it also draws attention away from the important role gender plays in building and sustaining relationship-based faith.[11]

Female Enclaves

The women's ministry programs at Bay Chapel and Mount Olive exhibit a curious emotional link to their respective congregations. At Mount Olive, where worshipers are discouraged from public display of charismatic "gifts of the Spirit," the central women's Bible study has women break out into individual groups of ten to twelve and physically separate from each other. As the study progresses, these often become "hot" groups, places of lavish charismatic expression, where women lay hands upon each other and pray aloud with fervent, rapid intensity. At Bay Chapel, where emotional displays during congregational worship are permitted (though not encouraged), women also break into small groups for intensive Bible study during Bible study programs, but these groups stay seated closely together in the same room for study, and their overall emotional tone remains significantly cool. These emotional links suggest that women's enclaves may function in an institutional emotional complementarity to congregations, though exploring that hypothesis is beyond the scope of this research.

In interviews, women consistently describe regular services as a time of passive listening. For my interviewees, real learning takes place in the all-female enclaves. Using all-female leadership, women's ministries provide Bible studies, spirituality retreats, and other specialized programming for women only—all of which encourage strong emotional bonds among women. As a result, there is not one symbolic universe within each congregation but two: the symbolic universe of the congregation and the symbolic universe of women. Since regular services symbolically shortchange female believers, many of them resorted to the enclaves, with the result that women's ministries flourished while men's remained minuscule.

In the symbolic universe of women, women lead as well as follow. As in the dominant symbolic universe, the Bible anchors intragroup authority, but in the symbolic universe of women, the leading Bible teacher is a woman: either a women's pastor, a pastor's wife, or a senior woman of the group. Thus, the enclaves provide a public arena for women's voices. Women rarely speak at congregational events. In the enclaves, only women speak and only women hear. The enclaves allow women to give and receive social validation for their ideas and experiences. This makes them places of powerful allure for women.[12] The resulting trust among women encourages the growth of substantial social relations among participants. Of the women I interviewed, most claim that three-fourths of their best friends are involved with the women's ministry programs at their congregation. At Bay Chapel and Mount Olive, women worship together, study the Bible together, and support each other in an attempt to live "a godly life." Thus, the female enclaves within these congregations function as a church within the church, a church created by and for women.

Reward, Compensation, and Gender?

At first glance, women's enclaves and the religious experiences they cultivate could be understood as a type of compensation that women generate in response to their exclusion from congregational rewards (Stark and Bainbridge 1985). To the extent that this is the case, gender at Mount Olive and Bay Chapel appears to be functioning much as class has historically. Due to the sacred wall of gender, women at Mount Olive and Bay Chapel possess scant ability to access the community's tangible rewards. At a minimum, the sacred gender walls support a social environment in which women are more likely to focus their energies on religious compensators and men on religious rewards, as Stark-Bainbridge define these terms.

Yet to view the Bay Chapel and Mount Olive women's enclaves through this interpretive lens one must posit fundamentalist women's religious experiences as something secondary, something that they turn to because this-worldly rewards are unavailable to them. This is a move warranted neither by the women's own understanding of the religious experiences they had (as articulated in interviews) nor by a reasonable amount of empirical evidence gathered in my field research. For instance, during my fieldwork numerous male believers expressed overt envy of women's religious gifts and the programming that helped cultivate them. By contrast, few women expressed any interest in being involved with male-dominated congregational administrative leadership. In taped interviews, only one woman—a member of Bay Chapel—mentioned access to leadership positions traditionally reserved for males as an important concern. In the course of this study, I was present at several enclave events to which men attempted to gain entry. During this same time period, no woman either claimed to be interested in attending male-only events or attempted to attend any meeting where only men were involved. Thus, to some men and many women, the ministries women are generating on their side of the sacred gender wall are a highly desirable good—to some, evidently, even more desirable than what men are generating on their side.

Intra- as well as extracongregational social ingredients may partially account for the one-wayness of this category envy. Intracongregationally, the sacred wall of gender allots men more power than women; thus, men can guard their sacred boundaries more readily than women and more firmly establish a social environment that discourages women from "crossing over." Extracongregationally, a disproportionate number of women held lower-status jobs that did not emphasize developing social contacts for advancement, thus removing some of the incentive for women to seek congregational rewards in Stark and Bainbridge's sense, thereby making congregational compensators a more attractive good.

In interviews, female believers spoke about religious experiences as the most desirable, tangible reward of faith and not as a compensator for the absence of material benefits. The desire for religious experiences was most women's primary motivator for their initial congregational involvement. Contra Stark and Bainbridge, fundamentalist women describe religious encounters as the *reward* they seek. Future studies comparing the religious values and experiences of female and male Christian fundamentalists might help us better ascertain the range and limits of congregational gendering practices in instigating gender-disparate ideas regarding the value of religious experiences among adherents, as well as whether and to what extent reward/compensation considerations may be involved.

Still, I continue to think that the women (and men) involved in these congregations are motivated by something more than sheer economic functionality. For further insight, it is necessary to return to the sacred canopy, its sacred gender wall, and consider the consequences of the intersection of two of its chief ideas—heterosexuality as a social norm and a male-imaged deity as a theological one—especially in terms of how these interact to shape the religious consciousness of believers in the gender-bifurcated life of a Christian fundamentalist congregation. For this strategic reflection, the work of Howard Eilberg-Schwartz offers valuable assistance. According to Eilberg-Schwartz, the imaging of the divine as monotheistic and the metaphors that spring from such a conception have had tremendous effect upon the religious imagination of the West. As the idea of a single deity slowly came to prevail among the ancient Jewish tribes, this deity was envisioned predominantly in male/father imagery. During this same time period, heterosexuality was strongly embraced as an important communal norm—not unusual among ancient peoples, for whom childbearing was a civic duty linked with survival (Eilberg-Schwartz 1994). The combination of these two developments—the acknowledgment of a chiefly male-imaged, solitary deity who commanded obedience and desired love from a people for whom heterosexuality had become a highly valued social norm—yielded an internally contradictory religious ethos for males. Men were expected to strive for closeness to a divine (mostly male-imaged) being whose mate was his people, yet they were

expected to do this without developing any homoerotic incli-
nations. As Christianity developed, it picked up and exacerbated this "male problem" of ancient Judaism by centering
upon the incarnation of the divine in Jesus, a human male. De-
fining the achievement of human salvation through an overtly
male figure as its central religious value, Christianity became
a religion marked by a "homoerotic dilemma generated for men
by Christ" (Eilberg-Schwartz 1994, 280).

While Eilberg-Schwartz is primarily concerned with the
impact of this religious dilemma on ancient Judaism, the sacred canopy over Bay Chapel and Mount Olive creates religious
communities that bear remarkable resemblance to the ancient
Jewish communities Eilberg-Schwartz describes. At Bay Chapel
and Mount Olive, pastors intentionally employ exclusively male
imagery for the divine. Further, each congregation's sacred
canopy includes communal norms that value heterosexuality
(expressed in marriage) and strongly censure homosexuality.
Consequently, both the emphasis on religious experiences in
the female enclaves and the dearth of religious experiences in
overall congregational life may be an entanglement of each
group's gender habits with its theological and social ideas rather
than a consequence of its gender-based social power conflicts.
The male-imaged deity and heterosexual norms integral to each
congregation's sacred canopy create an environment in which
women who seek religious experience are actually performing
their gender, while men perform theirs by declining to pursue
such conduct.

▨ *Summary and Conclusions*

"I'm not interested in religion but a relationship" is a central
metaphor that simultaneously expands and limits the faith of
Bay Chapel and Mount Olive women while revealing its con-
temporaneity. Denying history, it claims a postmodern privi-

lege of the personal. Critiquing religion is a hallmark of modernity. It has been pronounced psychologically an illusion of childhood wishes by Freud, derided as economically and politically obfuscatory by Marx, and identified as the ideological engine of capitalism by Weber. But critiquing a relationship is a slipperier task. A believer who invokes a relationship can disclaim potentially troublesome aspects of congregational life or polity as inessential to what really matters, because the pivotal event, her God relationship, is invariably tied to the details of her own life and therefore distinct from the actions and beliefs of her religious community.

While the claim of the women of Bay Chapel and Mount Olive that what they are involved with is "not religion but a relationship" provides them with a rhetorical shield against a sociohistorical deconstruction of their faith, the fact that what they admittedly are about is developing a relationship with a deity does not disqualify their activities as religion. On the contrary, it is a primary reason to describe them as such. Yet, such definitional quibbling does not trouble the believing women of Bay Chapel and Mount Olive. The theological looseness and lack of express concern they exhibit toward congregational belief and ritual norms communicates their commitment to individually grounded beliefs, even as the rigor with which they insist upon the reality of their God relationship testifies to their sincere conviction that they are genuinely interacting with the living God.

The gender dissonances among the sites generating the symbolic worlds of Bay Chapel and Mount Olive create critical openings that enable some women to assemble remarkably free interpretations of their religious experience. As the place where women can go whose symbolic needs are greater than regular worship can satisfy, the enclaves that make this freedom possible are also where women can escape from men, who frequently were responsible for the problems that got them involved with fundamentalism in the first place. To the tradition-prone women of Bay Chapel and Mount Olive, relationship Christianity offers an alternative meaning system that ameliorates some of the problems with that tradition that they are encountering. Emphasizing marriage and motherhood as primary sources of adult female identity, traditional gender patterns leave adult women at substantial identity risk in a period of high divorce such as the present. With its anchoring of adult identity in relationship to God, fundamentalist Christianity offered by contrast what appeared to godly women to be a safe harbor for the self—one in which the women I interviewed are gladly (though not always contentedly) taking shelter.

The Order of God

CHAPTER 5

Sex, Marriage, and Family Life

Although congregational services at Bay Chapel and Mount Olive are designed to facilitate and strengthen the bond between believers and their God, faith is only one emphasis of such second-wave Christian fundamentalist congregations. Decrying the American proclivity to separate religion from all other commitments, these youth-attracting religious institutions operate as a twentieth-century agora, periodically becoming a tumultuous public realm where culturally current issues are debated and resolved. The pastoral staffs of Bay Chapel and Mount Olive regularly speak out on local, state, national, and global issues—from abortion to foreign policy, from laws regulating homosexuality to the content of school textbooks—at congregational gatherings, with their stated goal to align the normative values of the congregation with what they understand to be God's order for the conduct of public and private social life.

Of the numerous issues raised during congregational meetings I attended at Mount Olive and Bay Chapel, gender roles, marriage, and the structure and meaning of the nuclear family received the most vigilant attention. Pastors claimed religious ground for their attention to these issues. Belief in a God-instituted order for human relationships is part of the sacred canopy that covers each congregation. The pastors insist that those who wish to live in accord with God's will for this world must replicate this order in their lives.

❧ Why Order?

A glance at the history of fundamentalist Christianity shows that the attention paid to gender and family issues by the pastoral staffs of Bay Chapel and Mount Olive is not novel. Instead, it is characteristic of Christian fundamentalism (DeBerg 1990; Bendroth 1993; Ammerman [1987] 1988). As Betty DeBerg has observed, the sermons and popular literature produced by fundamentalism's first leaders indicate that societal conflicts over gender and family issues were dominant issues for them as well (DeBerg 1990). An emphasis on gender and family issues is typical of conservative Christianity; it is one area where second- and first-wave fundamentalists remain aligned.

In light of this history, the relevant question to raise is not why the leaders at Bay Chapel and Mount Olive place so much emphasis on gender and family life issues but why their relatively young, well-educated congregants, Americans living in the late twentieth century, listen to what they have to say. For female believers express neither dismay at the quantity of congregational energy invested in gender and family issues nor (direct) discontent with most of the positions on these issues that their leaders take. Though as later portions of this chapter make evident, women's opinions on gender and family issues are significantly more nuanced than the public stands of their congregations, the women of Mount Olive and Bay Chapel are a receptive audience to congregational gender and family concerns. They welcome the attention paid to family life, and express considerable support for most of the teachings their churches provide. It is a critical consideration in evaluating this admittedly complex aspect of young women's involvement in second-wave Christian fundamentalist congregations to understand that female believers are not merely tolerating congregational norms on gender and family issues in obedience to pastoral authority. Many actively embrace them. The question is, Why? While causality is notoriously difficult to ascertain, one part of the answer appears to lie in the intersection of the women's autobiographies with contemporary cultural gender conflicts.

Preconversion Profiles and Demographics

Based on an overview of their profiles, I conclude that Bay Chapel and Mount Olive women believers have, as a group, been hit with the blunt edge of cultural conflicts over gender role norms—conflicts between work and the demands of parenting, between marital expectations and self-development, between faith and the rest of the world. The factors that place them in this uncomfortable position are their age, marital status, number and age of children, and amount of wage-earning employment. According to congregational surveys, 62 percent of those who attend Mount Olive are in the peak family development years of twenty-six to forty-five (see table 2).[1] At Bay Chapel, the figure is 72 percent. Overall, 49 percent of Mount Olive participants and 42 percent of those at Bay Chapel describe themselves as married and having never been divorced. Thirty percent of those from Mount Olive and 21 percent from Bay Chapel have children between the ages of five and twelve living at home. At each congregation, blended families combining children from previous marriages are a small but significant factor. Eighteen percent of participants at Mount Olive and 15 percent of those at Bay Chapel are remarried after having been

TABLE 2   ※ *Bay Chapel and Mount Olive Congregational Demographics*

	Aged 26–45	Married once	Total married	Household w/ children age 5–12	Divorced	Single
Bay Chapel	62%	49%	67%	30%	13%	16%
Mount Olive	72%	42%	60%	21%	12%	28%

divorced. Sixteen percent at Mount Olive and 28 percent at Bay Chapel indicate that they have never been married. Thirteen percent at Mount Olive and 12 percent at Bay Chapel are divorced and have remained single. The preponderance of young adults in the relatively early stages of work, careers, marriages, and parenting means that most of the people who belong to these congregations are currently involved in activities where contemporary changes in gender roles and the family are having their greatest impact. For the women who were the focus of this study, this was profoundly the case. Over half had converted during a period of marital crisis (see chapter 2). Sixty-two percent were engaged in some wage-earning work; of these, 32 percent worked full-time outside the home. According to Kosmin and Lachmin's surveys, this aligns them with the lowest rate of employment for religious women as a whole throughout the United States, who participate in the workforce either part-time or full-time at a rate ranging from 62 percent to 82 percent (Kosmin and Lachman 1993, 275–276). It appears likely, then, that because Mount Olive and Bay Chapel adherents are a population group situationally prone to experiencing gender and family frictions, they constitute a religious audience predisposed to pay attention to them.

Postconversion Expectations

An additional factor that boosts Bay Chapel and Mount Olive adherents' interest in gender and family issues also leaves them prone toward involvement in the parachurch political movement known as the New Christian Right (NCR). The soteriology inherent in the relationship-based conversion implies that an individual's life—once she or he converted—will change. "By their fruits ye shall know them," and one of the more significant fruits a believer can show is a life aligned with biblically based order.[2] According to Mount Olive and Bay Chapel pastors, the cornerstone of this order is heterosexual marriage headed by an adult male: a family. Congregational rhetoric emphasizes "the family" as the basic unit of an "orderly" world. Believers are encouraged to develop "family values" to cultivate God's order in the world.

This language (not coincidentally) overlaps with the rhetoric of the New Christian Right. Further research would be necessary to determine the extent of the interconnection between NCR groups and the Bay Chapel and Mount Olive congregations; however, conservative Protestant congregations like Bay Chapel and Mount Olive furnish the NCR with much of its grass-roots support. To the extent that Bay Chapel and Mount Olive adherents are attracted to NCR causes, it is likely that the NCR's rallying cry of family values and its attention to gender and family issues strike a resonant chord. Both are central components of Bay Chapel and Mount Olive religious life.

Congregational Teachings on Social Order

While both Bay Chapel and Mount Olive promote the idea that salvation is an individual experience, they also teach that the salvation drama takes place within a family unit. Ideally, the saved life is not lived alone but in the context of a nuclear family. Again according to "order," an individual's role in this family is determined by her or his sex and age. Adult female and male believers are expected to be married and within their marital relationship to enact complementary gender roles. The ideal family unit centers on a heterosexual complementarity of wife and husband in which the husband is the leader, the wife the follower. In this relationship, women derive value from their support of the spouse, care of the family home and childrearing (Ammerman [1987] 1988; Hunter 1987). Importantly, these norms of family order elevate gender—a relatively insignificant concern during conversion—into the pivotal factor of believers' daily lives.[3]

Field research on conservative Protestant congregations indicates that it is common for rhetoric condoning patriarchal family patterns to permeate community life. As a result, noticeable signs of community favor accrue to women involved with these congregations who demonstrate their compliance with the familial ideal (Ammerman [1987] 1988; Hunter 1987; Hardacre, in Marty and Appleby 1993). An excellent example of this is cited in Nancy Ammerman's *Bible Believers*. Engaged in ethnographic field research at a Southern Baptist fundamentalist congregation, Ammerman found that it was not until she herself became pregnant that important doors of communication within the congregation opened to her (Ammerman [1987] 1988, 113).

Gender and Marriage

The prevailing congregational rhetoric at Bay Chapel and Mount Olive insists that women and men are different from but necessary to each other. The situation is presented as a dilemma. While their need for each other mandates relationship, their differences yield perpetual conflict. The "ordered" answer to this dilemma is not for women and men to work things out for themselves, but to pattern their interactions with each other according to biblical mandates: heterosexual marriage between a complementary male/female believing pair is the foundation stone of earthly order.[4] Key to this order is the dominant role of men, known as "male headship." Men are expected to lead family life. But with this authority comes responsibility: husbands and fathers are responsible before God for the well-being and happiness of everyone else in the family. If a family member is miserable under a man's headship, then that man has failed in the proper exercise of his authority.

Order also pertains to the believing pair's interrelationship with their children and influences church life as well. Describing congregational teachings on order at Mount Olive, Sarah started by mentioning what it means within marriage, and then the family. Lastly, she mentioned the church as a site where God's order must prevail. "God has kind of set up an order. The husband is head of the home. This doesn't mean that he's the ruler of the home, but there's an order."

Those occupying the higher status in God's order for the world are not free to determine their behavior toward those below them. Their authority is limited by Bible teachings. Because of this, the pastoral staffs of Mount Olive and Bay Chapel invest considerable time teaching adherents how to be a family in accord with God's order for family life. They undertake this didactic task in three ways. One is through offering pastor-approved books and tapes on family order in the on-site congregational bookstore. A second is through sermons, teachings, and other authoritative public pronouncements dedicated to family order. The third way is teaching by osmosis, in that the normative order of the congregation models the patterns and rules of family life. What follows is a brief overview of each teaching method.

One of the simplest ways Bay Chapel and Mount Olive spread their message of God's order for gender and the family is the books, tapes, CDs, and videos in the sizable bookstore each church maintains. This made it easy for adherents to obtain educational materials explaining how religious familial order is supposed to work. At both congregations, these intracongregational shops are stocked with books, cassette tapes, videos, CDs, T-shirts, and posters offering pastor-approved advice on family life and gender. The bookstores include major sections on family life and marriage, where texts by authors such as James Dobson, president of Focus on the Family, and Charles Swindoll predominate.[5]

Bay Chapel and Mount Olive also familiarize adherents with gender and family norms through sermons, teachings, and the like. In a sermon on the family, Mike described submission between spouses as mutual. He also contended that the marital relationship was not the starting point of order. Initially, each person must be submitted to the creator God. "Husbands, submit to your wives. Wives, submit to your husbands. But before either of you do this, both of you submit to the Lord." Mike's depiction of mutual submission then turned into a commercial for a rapidly developing new Christian industry: Christian rock music. Mike stated that parents should go with their children to Christian rock concerts and "buy them Christian tapes if that's what they want." He also recommended that believing parents watch MTV with their children. "Then ask them, 'Do you think that's good?' Communicate with them. If you praise the Lord, they'll praise the Lord. They will imitate you." Mike's message again gives evidence of Mount Olive's alignment with specifically second-wave Christian fundamentalism. From the pulpit, he sanctions believers' engagement with contemporary culture—by, for instance, encouraging adherents to watch MTV with their children—as opposed to taking an adamant stand against it. Yet Mike also reinforces the standard fundamentalist message of patriarchal order. He encourages male believers to "praise the Lord" not only for the sake of their own God relationships but also for the sake of any children they may be rearing. Rory, at Bay Chapel, also takes strong stands on patriarchal order from the pulpit. When AB-101 (a bill banning the use of sexual preference as a ground for discrimination in housing or employment) came before the California state legislature, Rory preached against its passage and encouraged adherents to become actively involved in lobbying for its defeat.

While the patterns of congregational life and the texts in congregational bookstores set out clear, stringent ideals of gender and family life, the actual behaviors of real believers, including the pastoral staff, present a much messier picture. Traces of a softer order are also evident in pastoral sermons and teachings. At Mount Olive and Bay Chapel, a tendency to soften teachings on order became visible when the senior pastors drew from their personal experience to speak about family life. For both Pastor Mike and Pastor Rory had themselves experienced the trauma of a broken marriage. At Mount Olive, Mike and Elaine married in their late teens, only to divorce in their early twenties. A few years later, they remarried each other. In the interim, both had had children by nonspousal partners. Rory, the senior pastor at Bay Chapel, also has been divorced. He subsequently remarried, albeit to a different partner. These nonideal personal life histories affected the interpretations of gender and family order Mike and Rory were prepared to support. For instance, at either congregation, regardless of congregational ideals regarding the unity of order, a surprising variety of those who presented themselves as ordered families (traditional; divorced single parents; unwed women with children; married couples where one or the other or both had had previous marriages and children by those marriages) were recognized by Mike and Rory as proper Christian families and treated as such.

The third way Bay Chapel and Mount Olive teach adher-

ents about gender and family life is in congregational patterns
and rules. The ideal order for gender relations and family life
is reflected in institutionalized norms that circumscribe access
to authority depending upon one's sex (see chapter 3), by
church roles assigned by sex, and by senior pastor/pastor's wife
behavioral modeling. Males lead all mixed-sex groups; yet their
authority is not absolute. As in the ideal family order, male leaders are considered responsible before God for the well-being
of those under them. It is this responsibility, linked to their authority, that often leaves them open to considerable criticism.

At Mount Olive Mike instituted a rule that women with children under the age of eighteen could work for the congregation no more than twenty hours per week, but men with young
children may work full-time. One Mount Olive woman leader
who was part of the congregational staff told me, in confidence,
that the limit Mike had set on women's hours was controversial among female employees. Although the new rule stated that
women with young children could work for the congregation
no more than twenty hours per week, many were responsible
for tasks that required them to work well beyond that amount.
Since, however, the new congregational rule forbade them to
exceed twenty hours, the most consistent result was a reduc-
tion in women's pay rather than their hours. At Mount Olive,
female staffers with young children were continuing to do whatever was needed to get their jobs done but were paid for only
twenty hours per week, to avoid openly violating the policy.
Should criticism of the policy come to prevail, Mike would probably be accused of abusing his authority and required to make
amends.

Gender and family ideas are further ingrained in believers
through sex-linked ministries (see chapter 4) and parachurch
events. Mount Olive cooperates with several other Calvary
Chapels, for example, to sponsor a purity retreat for unmarried females. The central message of this event is that sexual-

ity is dangerous and must be hedged in by the rules of order. The event culminates in a moment when all unmarried females in attendance are asked to stand and pledge themselves to pre- marital sexual purity. At the retreat I attended, approximately twelve hundred young women took the pledge.

At Bay Chapel and Mount Olive, the idea that a God- ordered pattern governs relationships between women and men is powerfully reinforced in marriage rituals. Before a pastor will marry a couple at either church, the prospective bride and groom are required to attend a series of premarital counseling classes, in which they are taught their respective marital roles.

The architecture at Bay Chapel and Mount Olive teaches order as well. Each congregation had a nursing mothers' room, separated from the rest of the congregation by one-way glass, in which women could view the service while nursing without being publicly seen. The investment of congregational income for breast-feeding women conveyed a mixed architectural mes- sage regarding motherhood. Adjacent to the sanctuary, the room reminded believers of the tie they valued between women and infants; yet its separateness suggested that women literally en- gaged in infant nurture were an embarrassing sight. Women who recently had given birth were welcome to participate in com- munal gatherings; however, they could do so only in a special, isolated room, safely screened away. Even the sturdy pro- maternal stands of Bay Chapel and Mount Olive were insuffi- cient to remove the female breast from its status as a fetishized sex object in Western culture.

Family order concerning older children is communicated architecturally and programmatically. While adults participate in the central, regular services led by adult males, older chil- dren are separated out into various classrooms around the edges of the main sanctuary before regular services begin and offered children's church lessons taught by mixed-sex adult teams led by men. In the godly order taught by Bay Chapel and Mount Olive, high praise is given to adults who engage in child instruction as well as in childbearing and -rearing. In congregational life, both women and men take on the task of teaching the young.

Flexible Strictness

While order established boundaries between the self and chaos, it is not rigidly enforced in all directions. In matters of appearance—dress, cosmetics, jewelry, and comportment—Bay Chapel and Mount Olive permit considerable freedom. There is no endorsement for the decidedly antifeminist hyperfemininity of a Tammy Bakker. Nor is there support for a modern-day dress reform such as that in early fundamentalism (DeBerg 1990, 106). The consensus in these culturally current Christian fundamentalist congregations is that God accepts people however they are dressed. Order exists, but it has its limits. Personal appearance is one.

The Enclaves

When order fails, the enclaves or social networks of women are the principal sites in congregational life where women can be heard. They also function as emergency rooms for women experiencing severe marital discord. I was confronted with a concrete example of this during a Bay Chapel study one day. A woman new to the group broke into tears as soon as the women began their opening prayer. The night before, she told us, she had left her physically abusive husband and spent the night in her car. She came to the women's Bible study that morning because she did not know where else to go. The women sitting nearest her quietly put their arms around her and held her as she cried. A women's leader standing hearby invited her to stay at her home until more permanent arrangements could be made.

In addition to such physical assistance, enclaves also provided much-needed psychological support for many women. To
Judith, at Bay Chapel, this is what gives women's ministries
their appeal. "My sole purpose in going to a woman's ministry
was that there wouldn't be men there. I felt very safe personally, because there would be other women. It had nothing to
do with their age, their experiences, or anything else other than
that they were women."

Given the extensive difficulties women reported having with
their spouses, many perceived the all-female enclaves as a haven where they could momentarily escape from the dynamics
of gender and family life.

Congregations and Order

A rough translation of the gender messages implicit in the public
(i.e., mixed-sex, adult) patterns and rules that prevail at Bay
Chapel and Mount Olive is that the senior pastor is father to
the congregation, male congregants are his obedient sons, and
female congregants mostly facilitate the activities initiated and
led by males (serving as ushers to nursing women, contributing money, etc.). Since congregational rhetoric teaches adherents that the order of congregational life is applicable to the
home, these patterns convey an implied message regarding gender and family life: adult males should function as fathers,
younger men (if any are present) should act as obedient sons,
and females in the family, of whatever age, should facilitate the
activities of the males. Although oppositional opportunities are
present for women in the all female-enclaves (see chapter 3),
the patterns and rules of public activities provide a model for
family life consistent with a male-dominated, patriarchal authority pattern.

Enforced Heterosexuality

Where Mount Olive sponsored special instruction for female believers on how to address homosexuals and confront homosexuality, Bay Chapel confines its rhetoric on homosexuality and homosexuals to the pulpit. Since a patriarchal heterosexual family unit is the form in which the ideal saved life occurs, homosexuality is not an acceptable lifestyle alternative at either Bay Chapel or Mount Olive. Seen as disrupting the establishment of the God-ordered male/female complementary pair, it is solidly condemned. The pastoral staff instruct believers that it is a contradiction for anyone to claim to be Christian and homosexual. At one Wednesday night Bible study I attended, Mike spoke of homosexuality as evil but indicated that believers are still required to love homosexuals, in keeping with the movement's consistent love ethic. "We hate what they do, but we love them. Don't accept evil. Don't accept something against God's will, but love everyone."

Love, however, does not require socializing with homosexuals. At a Mount Olive women's meeting, the women's leader, Virginia, gave those present detailed instructions on how to confront women they suspected to be lesbian. "Go up to any woman who gives you the eye and ask, 'Are you gay?' If she says, 'Yes,' you are to say, 'I'm a Christian, and the way I believe, personally, it's wrong. Keep your eyes off me.'" A woman present then asked, "So we should avoid even social situations?"—to which Virginia responded, "Yes. Don't go to anything." Virginia confessed to the group that her sister is a lesbian. She said that she loves her sister but not what she does. The condemnation of homosexuality she prescribed for women was absolute. "If you accept homosexuality, you won't stop at anything. Even murder," she claimed. In accord with patriarchal norms, Virginia treated men as central to her topic—even when the subject was lesbianism. She accomplished this by linking lesbian sexuality with male abuse rather than female desire.

"Some of us who have been horribly hurt by men think men are no good. So, we get involved with women. The Holy Spirit is telling you it's wrong. The Bible says it's not normal. Jesus makes us functional. You need to say, 'I was a victim,' then grieve it and drop it at the Lord's feet." Virginia explained to the group that Christian parachurch organizations existed that helped people who were "trying to get out of the life." Organized like Alcoholics Anonymous, Cocaine Anonymous, and other Twelve-Step groups, each had an 800 telephone number that those prone to lesbian, bisexual, or gay behavior could use to reach help if they found themselves attracted to a person of the same sex. "It's a Christian organization that helps lesbians and gays get out. They form a tight family—like a gang. They do everything together, so it's hard to get out." Virginia urged those present to give the 800 number to any friends or relatives who "might need it."

In an odd reversal, the antihomosexual activism of Bay Chapel and Mount Olive is a sign of the increased social and political visibility homosexuals have achieved. When homosexuals are closeted, there is little catalyst for fundamentalists to organize against them.

Women's Ideas about Order and Moral Life

In any religious group, the correlation between a leader's public rhetoric and an individual believer's ideas is never absolute. Since women enjoy only a minor role in the production of public rhetoric at Bay Chapel and Mount Olive, a sizable gap between congregational rhetoric and women's beliefs—particularly on gender and family issues—might reasonably be expected to exist. Paradoxically, this proved both to be and not to be the case.

Gender

Bay Chapel and Mount Olive women often respond obliquely or evasively to express queries on the subject of gender. To obtain comments on gender-related issues, I had to probe for them around women's androgynous-seeming primary religious orientation.[6] Mary, on staff at Mount Olive as Elaine's assistant and a dedicated adherent as well, gives voice to what she believes is the significance—or rather, the insignificance—of gender to a believer. "We have all found our freedom in Christ, and we know that we are all one in Christ. There is no difference between—like Scripture says, between Greek or Jew, between male or female. There is no difference."

Yet, in direct contradiction to this express belief in unity, once women did talk openly about gender, they invariably proclaimed that women are women, men are men, and the two are different. The largely positivistic stance women take toward gender sounds much like a carryover from their Scottish commonsense-realism approach to the Bible. Just as the Bible says what it means and means what it says, to Bay Chapel and Mount Olive women it is clear who women and men are and what they should do, for the Bible tells them. In its pages, they read a story of order. Before God and in heaven, women and men are spiritually equal; but on earth, in their relationships to each other, women and men are different. They have distinct roles to enact, different duties to perform.

To the women I interviewed, a female believer is, as a believer, equal to any male believer in her relationship with God; however, in daily life, her femaleness determines the range of relational possibilities available to her. Women both assumed transcendent gender equality and, to varying degrees, accepted immanent gender difference. Molly, Mike's secretary at Mount Olive and an active women's ministry participant, describes this dichotomy as one of faith versus roles. "When Jesus came, he made it really clear that men and women were the same to him.

They have the same value. They are the recipients of the same salvation. There was no difference to *him*. The potential was there for equality in that sense, not necessarily in position but in *true* equality. Men and women have different roles. They have different roles in the church. They have different roles in the home. They have different responsibilities."

Louise identifies the similarities and differences between women and men somewhat differently. Where Molly understands Jesus as a historical figure who clarified women and men's salvific equality and describes gender roles without giving them a transcendent ground, Louise credits God with establishing gender differences from the beginning of time. "We're all people. We all have a need for love, acceptance. Spiritually, we all have the need to be saved. We are the same in God's eyes. We are all his children. But God has given us different roles. I know that from the Bible. I read it in his Word."

At Bay Chapel, Judith regularly complains to the pastoral staff about the lack of balance between women's and men's programming. She is pleased with the congregation's support for women's programming but thinks it is equally important for men to be structurally encouraged to fulfill their leadership role.

> I see such a lack. I said to the staff here, "You have one woman's pastor and everything with women." I said, "You have fifteen men pastors and nothing for men. Why?" [Q: What did they say?] They changed everything. The men are now having Bible studies. They have men's accountability groups. They have more things for men. They said, "The foundation is women." I said, "But it's wrong. The foundation should be men. The men should be leading." The men don't want to take responsibility for society, for the church. Men are running away from marriages. They're running away. They won't get married. They're scared of society, of life itself. Even when they're not in the church, of life, itself. It's like they are saying, "I don't

want to get married and have kids. Life is too hard." Even in church, men's number-one struggle is with responsibility. They are scared of that word.

Judith's comments highlight an important gender concern for Bay Chapel and Mount Olive women. They are avidly interested in having men fulfill their gender roles in the congregation and in their homes. Like a waltz, a gender complementarity only works when both partners take the appropriate steps. As women, they can only successfully follow godly order if men follow it too.

Godly Women and the Family

Elaine's talk on saving families by prayer, cited in chapter 1, gets to the heart of Bay Chapel and Mount Olive women's relationship to their families. One of the fiercest criticisms of modernity they make is that the individuality it exalts goes against godly order. Though they express some flexibility about exactly what a family is, to them, the family, not the individual, is the basic unit of human community. In terms of their role within this family unit, female believers claim they want to be godly women: women submissive to God who "didn't really live of this world," as Kiersten phrases it. In persistent humility, no female believer ever claimed to be a godly woman; to do so would have been deemed an act of pride. Instead, "godly woman" is an honorary status, a form of recognition conferred by the believing community in response to a woman's consistent commitment to her faith.

Though being a godly woman is a common aspiration for female believers, Mount Olive and Bay Chapel women differ in what they think is necessary to achieve it. For example, Jane, a young professional who had attended Bay Chapel for twelve years, disputes the idea that ordered gender roles are an essential component.

Our stereotype, our guideline for life, our plumb line is the word of God. God's word does not say that the wife has to be cooking and cleaning and doing housework, while the husband is the breadwinner. It says, love without hypocrisy, be devoted to one another in love and good deeds. It doesn't talk about roles, except for the fact that the wife needs to have a quiet spirit or something and the husband needs to love his wife as Christ loved the church. There are certain commands, but they are not task-specific in the Bible.

Married for twenty-two years and one of the few African Americans at Bay Chapel, Barbara claims that gender roles have nothing to do with God's order. While indicating that some differences between women and men probably do exist, to Barbara they are much smaller than can be inferred from prevailing gender roles. "There are roles for men and women, but I don't see the need for them. Most of the time, a man can do the same thing a woman can do. There are some things a woman cannot do, and there are some things a man cannot do; but the things that they both can do, I don't see why they can't be shared." Like Barbara, Sonia, a Mexican-American member of Bay Chapel, also considers gender roles social conventions and claims they are largely interchangeable between women and men—especially where the hard work of parenting is involved. "My dad was always there for us. He would be the coach in our lives. He was the one who always coached me in sports and stuff, and my brothers also. That was his area, and my mom would be the supportive one. Now sometimes I feel like I'm the coach. There are other times when I see my husband being the coach. We support that, because he knows how to coach in certain things and I know how to coach in other things." Sonia also does not see a "family" as necessarily including children. "A husband and wife without children are a family. Sometimes people don't look at it that way, but I certainly do."

Yet these three women are exceptional. Their ideas stand in stark contrast to a looming consensus among the other women I interviewed. Most declared that the spiritual goal of becoming a godly woman requires one to fit into a particular, biblically mandated gender-complementarity role. The biggest disagreement among women is not over whether gender roles are part of a godly order; almost all think they are. Where they disagree is over why this is so, that is, over the sacral etiology of gender. Some consider the prescription of gender roles a pragmatic move on the part of a creator God, a partitioning of labor and responsibility instigated by their God to facilitate necessary things getting done. Others claim that gender roles are an integral aspect of existence, that a creator God built them into everyone, and thus that gender roles reflect inherent, essential differences between women and men.

After thirteen years at Mount Olive, Molly favors the pragmatic explanation. "Women and men have been assigned different roles. That doesn't make one higher, one lower. They're all equal in God's eyes, but that doesn't mean everybody does the same job." Cory, also active at Mount Olive for thirteen years, considers gender roles an aspect of godly order in much the same way Molly does. To Cory, gender roles are pragmatically useful tools of socialization rather than absolutes. For Cory, gender roles were included in godly order to ease relations between women and men; therefore, gender roles are authoritative only to the extent that they help men and women make decisions together and are not ends in themselves. "I think that the husband should be the leader of the house, but the wife should be so close to him that basically, even if they don't always agree exactly on how something should be handled, they are close enough to compromise, so they can deal with the situations that arise in the home." Louise, involved with Mount Olive for nineteen years, tends to believe there are essential differences between women and men but claims that cultural customs may have partly influenced her commonsense understanding. "Their makeup is different. With guys and girls, what is more important to them differs. Guys are more physical. Women are more emotional. Guys are always, it seems, into the physical things, women into all the sentimental things that mean more. It could be there are real differences. It could be, but I don't know. I really don't know if that's a woman thing in general, or if that's our culture." Louise relativizes complaints regarding the disadvantages American women experience by arguing that women in the United States are better off than women anywhere else in the world.[7] "In America, we got it really good as women. I can't believe that women sit around and cry about it. There are so many places that women are still considered about as good as a dog. . . . One time it really hit me was when I went on one ministry tour with my husband to Egypt. Women had to walk around with scarves over their faces. . . . They were like nonpeople. They acted, like, 'Step out of the way. Here comes a guy.' Here, women can do anything they want."

Singleness

Mount Olive and Bay Chapel women have almost nothing to say, certainly nothing laudatory, about being single. Their own marital status and age may be partially implicated in this silence. All but a handful are married; among the married, most are in the first decade of married life and had been primed for conversion by marital trauma (see chapter 2). The challenge of achieving a well-functioning marriage occupied the attention of Bay Chapel and Mount Olive women, both married and single. To both, singleness is not a desirable lifelong option. At best, it is an interim state that, with God's blessing and in accord with God's timing, is rapidly brought to a close.

Women contextualize their high valuation of marriage and

family by describing it as a way they are attempting to align themselves with godly order and preserve traditional values; yet, historically, their focus is a quite modern one—particularly for Christians. Initially, part of Christianity's appeal to women was that it offered them an alternative to marriage. Through its sanction of celibate life, Christianity provided an alternative vocation for (upper-class) women (Schussler-Fiorenza 1990). Even as late as the early twentieth century, the educational, missionary, and congregational institutions of conservative Protestantism were places where single women could work in positions of greater responsibility than they could hope to obtain in any secular job (Bendroth 1993, 88). By the late twentieth century things began to change.

At Bay Chapel and Mount Olive, few options for single women exist. This is because, theologically and socially, marriage is the norm. Few programs or social events and little congregational rhetoric is available to believers should they desire to contradict it and pursue a norm of single blessedness. At Bay Chapel, Teresa, the lone unmarried female staffer, led the one single women's Bible study sponsored by the church. Yet her ministry, though small, impressed Judith, the married, Mexican-American leader of Bay Chapel's Thursday night women's ministries, to articulate support for singleness.

> In the Psalms, Christ talks that you should multiply and be fruitful. You should live out your heritage. It's having a destiny, having someone to continue your life generation to generation, Christian to Christian. [Yet] there is a place [in the Bible] where Paul speaks about women being single and Christian. If you were married, you couldn't do all that you could do for Christ if you were single, because married you have to think of a husband. If you're single, you could do more. You could go on missionary trips. It's your life with Christ. What are you doing with it? Are you just sitting home doing nothing? Why are you single?

Even so, Judith is not as supportive of singleness as Paul of Tarsus, who considered it the preferable way to live (1 Corinthians 7:1–9). For Judith and her godly sisters, remaining single is acceptable only if one remains unwed to dedicate one's libidinal energy to the service of God.

At Mount Olive and Bay Chapel, antiabortion activism also can take an oblique form, such as in congregational behavior toward single pregnant women. Mount Olive supports a sizable adoption ministry. When Alice, a single parent worshiping at Mount Olive, wanted her child dedicated, the congregation extended full public rites to her two-month-old infant son, Montana. The day Mike announced the baby dedication, he invited Alice to bring Montana up on the stage—with no father present. Mike explained to the congregation, "Alice understands she's promising to raise her child in the Lord. She's a single mother, so Alice needs special support. Our prayer is that Montana will grow up to be a man of God." After Pastor Mike uttered a brief, inaudible prayer over the baby, he handed Alice a dedication certificate. The congregation applauded for almost a full minute. No mention was made of the baby's father. As Alice returned to her seat with Montana in her arms, a family member took a photo of the two, mother and child, leaving the stage. In light of the strong antiabortion stand at Mount Olive, the social meaning of Mike's public dedication of Montana and public support for Alice is fairly clear. Without doubt, it was not a sign of congregational support for women's singleness, or for sexual freedom—though, it is reasonably possible that some of those in attendance might have read it that way. Mike probably intended it as a symbolic stand against abortion, a center-stage ritual designed to encourage women to carry pregnancies to term rather than have abortions.

❋ *Order between Wives and Husbands*

While Bay Chapel and Mount Olive women see faith as grounded in the experience and commitment of an individual, they claim that an individual's faith is best lived out in a complementary marital relationship. Singleness, while acceptable, is not desirable. Being in a committed, marital relationship is integral to living in accord with God's order. The word women employed to describe how spouses living in accord with godly order should interrelate is "submission."

To Mount Olive and Bay Chapel women, submission is applicable to all aspects of marriage; yet its precise meaning is field-dependent. What submission means varies considerably, depending upon the facet of marriage involved. Four areas of marital life that expose the range of meanings associated with submission are daily interactions, sexuality, major decisions, and overall marital status. For the first two areas of marital life, submission is supposed to be mutual. In daily life and in their sexual relationship, a wife and husband are to submit to each other. Balance is the goal, and thus submission is equally binding upon the actions of both. But when it comes to making major decisions such as whether to move out of state or buy a house, or when it comes to bearing responsibility for the overall success of a marriage, submission is described very differently. In these areas, submission is a marital dynamic in which husbands take the lead and make decisions to which their wives "submit"; yet, this decision-making power has a sacred catch. The husband who exercises it simultaneously becomes responsible to God for his wife's response to the decision he has made. If his decisions are selfish and make his wife angry or sad, he will, women insist, have to answer to God for the hurt he has inflicted.

Nancy, at Bay Chapel, describes submission much as Mike does, albeit in more colorfully descriptive language. To her, submission is a marital ideal applicable to both partners.

Submission is a mutual thing. It's like two puzzle pieces that fit together. My best friends, when they talk about their marriage, they don't have a whole lot of fights and conflicts. I asked them once, "How do you guys do that? I know you're not faking it. I know you're not shoveling the conflict underneath." The way she voiced it—it's always stayed with me—was that part of Ephesians where it says, "Husbands, love your wives as Christ loved the church, willing to lay your life down for her," and then, "Wives, submit yourselves to your husbands." That is mutual submission. The husband theoretically can't be overbearing, the way the world sees submission. So I've not seen submission in the marriage relationship as onerous or an awful thing . . . if you are in a mutual submission situation.

Involved with Bay Chapel for twelve years and married for seven of them, Jane describes herself and her marriage in terms of family and marital order, with her marriage an exercise in mutual submission.

I am definitely feminine and my husband is definitely masculine, but that doesn't necessarily mean that I'm the domestic homemaker/cooker/sewer/housecleaner and he's the breadwinner who sits in a Lazy Boy chair watching sports on television while I serve him grapes. We have a mutually submissive relationship. He gives everything he can. I do everything I can.

Lesley, an active Mount Olive participant, who has been married six years and is pregnant with her second child, does not perceive submission as mutual. She considers it her unique responsibility, as part of marital order, to submit to her husband. Her husband's role, she insists, is far more demanding than the one she has to fulfill.

I think it says, "Wives, submit to your husbands; and husbands, love your wives as Christ loved the church." Well, Christ died for the church. So I really think it means my husband would be literally willing to die for me—not so much physically, but by going to work everyday he is putting down a part of his life. . . . He works a lot of extra hours that maybe he wouldn't do. He's doing it for the good of the family. For me and for the baby. Not for himself. I think, really, he has it a lot harder than I do. It would be easier to submit than to literally give up your whole life for something.

Martha, who has been attending Mount Olive for four years and who credits her and her husband's conversion with saving their troubled marriage, seconds Lesley. Martha embraced submission for herself because marital order placed upon her husband the bulk of the responsibility to sustain their marital tie.

We believe in the headship of the male. We believe that that's a biblical principle, and I accept that. As a woman in marriage, it is kind of neat on the one hand, because he's more responsible than I am. He is responsible before the Lord.

Ann, a Bay Chapel adherent for ten years, describes family order as a God-sanctioned prioritizing process that begins at home but stretches out to encompass the federal government.

We're back to God, God's standards for authority. God first, the husband second, the mother next, and then the children. I think the government and their agencies are to serve that unit. Not the other way around.

Ann's facile reference to men as husbands and to women as mothers reveals a crucial component of the philosophical roots of order. To those for whom godly order is a viable religious tenet, individuals possess no inalienable connection to the divine but instead become acceptable to God only by aligning themselves with the structures of godly order and participating in ordered relationships with each other.

For Lesley, the teachings on order she was exposed to in

women's ministry meetings convinced her to work on improv-
ing her troubled marriage, something general congregational
teachings and the counseling advice of a male pastor failed to
achieve.

> My husband didn't want to split up, but I had just had it with
> him. I went to counseling [with a Mount Olive pastor], and
> he counseled me not to leave. I said, "That's too bad. I'm leav-
> ing anyway." Right after counseling, I went to the women's
> Bible study. The teaching of the day was how God says no in
> three different ways. I was nailed. It was like, "No. You can't
> leave." I thought, Oh great; now I have to stay with him. So I
> went home and told him . . . "We'll try it again." We've had our
> ups and downs since then, but I don't think we're anything
> out of the ordinary. And things are better.

As Lesley's story illustrates, fundamentalist women do not solely
draw upon the symbolic resources of women's ministries to help
them achieve what they assess to be personally desirable ends.
Like Lesley, most of the women I interviewed treat the symbolic goods they encounter in the enclave as faith resources
that can, if sufficiently effective, help them critically evaluate
the life choices they make.

When Louise speaks about the contemporary move toward
gender egalitarianism, she does not sweepingly depict it as inherently bad. What concerns her is that the move toward gender equality may interfere with the goals of biblical order. To
Louise, God's commands must take precedence over everything,
even the contemporary equation of justice with equal rights.

> Women are getting more and more rights each day as we go
> along, practically, you know. Now it's not just women.
> Everybody's fighting for their rights. In biblical times, women
> were not thought of as highly as they are now. In history,
> women have gained more status, more rights. A hundred years

ago, we couldn't vote. I personally think they are carrying it way too far. In the house where I grew up, my mom ran it. I was raised that way. It's inbred in me, this rebellious "You're not going to tell me what to do, *man*, just because I'm a woman." But biblically, it refers to us as the weaker vessel. Women are people. They are people, but they're asking for so many things. They want to be equal. I feel we're losing many advantages as women. I like the niceties. I like being treated respectfully. I like somebody saying, "Oh, don't talk that way. There's a woman present."

Divorce

The tie between earthly marriage and God's order creates strong taboos around divorce. While separation is acknowledged as a viable strategy to preserve a marriage, divorce is always an undesirable alternative. The two conditions women cited as being adequate grounds for divorce are physical abuse and drug or alcohol abuse—not, rather amazingly, the traditional Christian grounds of adultery. While it was neither accepted nor condoned, adultery (if the adulterous spouse was repentant) is a marital problem women believe can be resolved. They consider physical abuse and drug or alcohol abuse much less amenable to resolution. Judith claims that God does not want violence between spouses and will work to stop it by putting people in the couple's path that pull the two apart.

> If the husband or wife was physically abusing the other continuously and it never stopped, I think that they should separate. That family, the community should step in to separate them. Usually the husband or wife won't leave the situation. I think community should come in. [Q: How?] It will always be different. It just depends on how violent the husband is. If he has shotguns around, you can't be unwise as to what you're doing. You get authorities. You call in the police. You do some-

thing. A lack of response is like shutting your eyes and shutting your ears, that nothing's happening. That's just as damaging as the person living through it. I feel God has put you in this position. You should ask, Why did you see it? There's a reason why: because that person needs you to step in for them, because they can't. They can't make decisions, because they are frozen. They are nonthinking.

Note that Judith did not describe the duty of intervention as limited to believers. Marital abuse is a form of human violence that demands community and institutional action. Relatedly, Bay Chapel and Mount Olive women unanimously claim that marital rape is possible and voice strong support for the passage of marital rape laws.

Single Women's Views on Marriage

In an intriguing turn of events, unmarried female believers articulate a strongert pro-male stance than married women and show great affinity with the women converting to Orthodox Judaism studied by Lynn Davidman (Davidman 1991). Linda, a Bay Chapel member who is divorced and has not yet remarried, flatly supports male leadership and condones male assertiveness. She worries that the societal struggle to secure equal rights for women and men is undermining men's capacity to develop the strong masculine identities she prefers. "With the women being more aggressive nowadays and wanting equal rights, that is part of what created the problem of men not being as assertive anymore as they used to be. I want to see men being more assertive." Vicky, an unmarried Mount Olive participant, describes men as serving a priestly role in the home, where they stand between women and God. In marriage, Vicky claims, a wife is supposed to support her mate, but a husband is, in return, responsible for his wife's development. "There are different roles in the home. The husband is the mediator between the family and God. It is his responsibility to guide the family. It is his responsibility to take care of his wife, to provide for her happiness, to provide for her needs. She is, in a sense, what he makes her to be. That's his responsibility. A wife is there to be a helper, an encourager, a supporter, a prayer partner, a prayer warrior for her husband."

Initially I found it curious that married female believers on the whole discuss marriage in relatively egalitarian terms, describing submission in soft-order language as a mutual dynamic, while single female believers depicted marriage in the hard-order language of male dominance. My tentative hypothesis is that hard-order metaphors may function as a critical trope in dating and courtship language, exhibiting a female believer's readiness for an ordered marital tie. But once marriage occurs and an actual marital relationship is underway, the hard-order discourse of courtship gets overwritten by lived experiences. Being there makes all the difference.

Parenting

To Rachel, the Bay Chapel mother of a five year old, parenting is a major challenge, and godly order the path through it. "It's become such an open world. Now is the time when we should teach our children individually as Christians and raise them up in right values. No one else is going to do it. . . . I know she is going to do wrong. She may be one of the kids that gets pregnant when she's fifteen. I want to be there for her, to support her, to say, 'Yes. It's okay. God forgives you. We're gonna make the best of it and we are going to go on.'" Sandra, an upper-middle-class, married, active participant at Mount Olive, is the mother of two teenage children. She runs her own interior design business and serves as a women's Bible study leader. When asked "What is the most important issue facing Christian women today?" Sandra immediately mentions mothering. To Sandra, her high valuation of mothering—for which she receives significant support at Mount Olive—is a countercultural, anticapitalistic act. "The most important issue facing Christian women today is the role of the <u>woman in terms of her obligation as a mother. That's probably</u> her strongest and most important role. For the world, probably the least important; for the Christian woman, the most important. For the world, it's the least important because it has no *value*. It doesn't make money. It doesn't make a statement. It's just drudgery, and drudgery, and drudgery."

Yet where Sandra finds support in her faith for the commitment she makes to mothering, other married women told me their faith relativizes the importance of their role as mothers. Sara, a Mount Olive participant in her midtwenties who is the mother of two toddlers, explains, "If you have your children as idols, God will tolerate this only so long. A mother may be willing to lay down her life for her children and grandchildren, but this cannot get in the way of a woman's first commitment—to God." Thus, to some women, their relationship-based faith means that a believer's connection with God must come before anyone or anything else. This includes children. For female believers, while mothering is important, it should not be the primary source of personal identity.

Ann describes her moral framework in stark, individualist terms; she is a moral Clint Eastwood. Ann is a veteran of disagreements with school authorities over mandatory vaccinations, a practice with which she forcefully disagrees. That she has had to argue with school authorities to do what she wants with her own children is, to Ann, merely one small example of the erosion of order under way in society.

I use standards that don't change, based on the Scriptures. I have moral absolutes. The majority of the population doesn't even think they exist. I think that we really have the Bible as a standard in life. You don't steal. You don't murder. You don't hurt people. You don't sleep with people before you're married. You respect other people's property. You put other people's needs above your own. Well, if those are my standards, I'm certainly not going to give people free rein to my children who have standards completely opposed to those. I think that's my right as a parent. I know there are certain legislators who think that children's rights are more important than parents' rights, but not mine.

Ann contends that family order is a societal problem rather than something individually based. To Ann, people's values are adrift in the United States. They go into debt for material goods and then have to work extra hours to pay off that debt, hours that would otherwise have been spent with their families. Ann considers it deeply wrong for people to cherish material goods more than their own children.

Society as a whole places value on things that don't have as much value and places little value on things that really do have the value. Children have the value. Things aren't the value. But, as a whole we're a society of debt. So people have to go to work to make money to pay the debt. I'm not saying that they shouldn't pay the debt, but as a whole those years at home with the children are not held up [to be] as valuable as making the money to have things.

At Mount Olive, Mary describes the battle that some fundamentalists wage with public schools and other institutions over the way their children are treated as an outgrowth of the paramount value fundamentalists place upon their faith. "We want children to be trained up according to Scripture and the ways of the Lord rather than man-made doctrine. In our heart of hearts, we feel that that's what the Lord would have us to do."

At Bay Chapel and Mount Olive, women's social networks are a human resource women can tap when they have questions about parenting. Sometimes this entails seeking assistance over relatively mundane matters, such as the best shoes to buy for a hyperactive toddler but they also provide a social safety net for women in parenting crises. At a Bay Chapel retreat prayer meeting, a woman who suspected her ex-husband was sexually abusing their young daughter broke into a wail of public agony that rocked the room. "Oh, Father, hear my cry. My daughter is only three years old. The law is not helping me. The courts are not helping me. Protect her from the evil one. I don't know what else to do, Father, but cry to you. Hear my cry, I pray. You know what's going on." Immediately after she began this prayer, the two women sitting next to her quickly put their arms around her shoulders. As the prayer continued, another woman, who had been sitting some distance away, got up, walked over to the distressed woman, knelt before her, and put her arms around her waist. Others remained where they were but began to cry. Slowly, the group processed the complex, powerful emotions that the woman's prayer of agony had unleashed. When the prayer session ended, enclave leaders approached the woman and started working with her to discover and address her concrete needs and consider the legal and behavioral steps necessary to assure her child's safety. Thus the enclave provided a public space where a woman could air her most pressing parenting concern, and then the physical, emotional, intellectual, and economic resources to help her cope with it.

Abortion

According to Rebecca Klatch's study of women of the New Right, morally conservative religious women are a major political force in the lobbying efforts to block use of public funds to pay for abortions, as well as in the disruption of abortion clinics through bodily blocking access to them (Klatch 1987). Yet at Bay Chapel and Mount Olive, few women are active in this effort. Elaine publicly speaks against abortion frequently in the women's Bible study sessions at Mount Olive, but at both congregations, contradictions and ambiguities between believers' ideas and official congregational norms on the issue of abortion abound. During the course of this study, the pastoral staff at Bay Chapel made Operation Rescue leave their premises. According to Operation Rescue staffers, they were asked to leave by the pastoral staff because Bay Chapel adherents offered little support for the organization. Within the Bay Chapel female enclave, a rumor prevailed that Operation Rescue was asked to leave because its leadership did not take a clear public stand against the violence of antiabortion activists.

When Mount Olive leaders tried to build support for the antiabortion cause by offering a training session on how to picket abortion clinics, only twenty-four people (out of a congregation of four thousand) showed up. Eighteen were women; six were men. None of the women who came were involved in any way in women's ministries. When it was time to start the meeting, the elderly woman who had organized the training session went up to the podium, looked at the small gathering before her, and said, "Pro-life isn't a real popular ministry." The crowd nodded in response. At Mount Olive and Bay Chapel pro-life is supported by the pastoral staffs but generates very little enthusiasm among mainstream believers.

Carol, a major leader of fundamentalist women's ministries in southern California, is extremely articulate about the conflicts within fundamentalism over abortion. She understands the gap as being between congregational rhetoric on abortion versus the experience of women who must actually confront the issue.

> About abortion. I think that's one of the hardest issues of the day. I understand a line of "No abortion is ever right," [but] if

I were faced with a rape and were pregnant, I know if I could have the washout in twenty-four hours, I would do that, before the egg was fertilized. I don't know what I would do about carrying [such a pregnancy to term]. I could sit with you and say, "I would not have an abortion." [But] I don't know what I'd do. I really don't. So it's one thing to say, "All abortion is sin." It's another thing to be faced with the issue. I've had friends who were faced with it. I was with a girl who was raped. She needed support, and I wanted to support her. I didn't want to say, "This is wrong." I didn't.

Still, Carol's ability to ponder moral ambiguity in relation to abortion is limited to women who want to terminate a pregnancy caused by rape. The more common abortion scenario, that of a married woman with children who might desire to abort a pregnancy for economic reasons or to preserve her physical or emotional health remains outside the reach of Carol's moral imagination.

Rachel, a twenty-five-year-old member of Bay Chapel, describes abortion in the terms that most of my interviewees use.

I don't believe in abortion. I believe there are other ways. Through prayer, God is with you always. So abortion, I don't think, should be an alternative, because God will take care of you. . . . My beliefs are what I believe for me. As far as anyone else, I can't tell you what to do. I can only say that I could be there as a support. If you wanted to have an abortion, have an abortion. I don't believe it's right, but that's my belief. If you needed support, I'm gonna be there to help you no matter what. That's just how I feel.

These findings support Wade Clark Roof's contention that the monolithic portrayal of conservative Christians as starkly antiabortion is erroneous. When it comes to the issue of whether women should be able to obtain a legal abortion, conservative

Christians in the baby boomer cohort exhibit "a greater mix of opinions than [is] often realized" (Roof 1993, 114). Only one of the women I interviewed—a woman in her sixties—belonged to a women's parachurch organization that regularly lobbies against abortion rights. On the other hand, 50 percent of the women were presently or had once been involved with Women's Bible Fellowship, a national parachurch organization that offers Bible studies for women. Contra much public perception, fundamentalist women are willing to go outside their congregations for more Bible study, but not to make political statements about abortion.

▓ *The Limits of Order*

The influence of the contemporary women's movement can be seen in the near total consensus among Bay Chapel and Mount Olive women that complementary roles apply only to family and church life. When it comes to (nonchurch) work, school, and politics, they concur that women and men are equals and should be paid and promoted without discrimination. Their only serious reservation concerned working women who have young children. Bay Chapel and Mount Olive women adamantly insist that young children require and deserve significant maternal and paternal attention. While acceptable for child care to come from others, it is their preference that children be reared by their parents.

In some tension with this parenting goal, both married women and men need to work outside the home, fundamentalist women claim. Lesley's words best sum up this sentiment. "Everyone has to work these days, just to get by," she claims. This tension leads women to take some progressive stands on workplace gender issues. The women unanimously support mandatory paid maternity leave for women. But this commitment does not seem to extend very far. Curious as to whether believers' progressive commitment to equal parenting extended into the workplace, I queried several women about whether they would support paternity leave as well. The responses I collected were lukewarm at best. None had ever heard of the idea before I mentioned it, and the most frequent response I got to my inquiry was a grave concern over whether employers could afford such a benefit (a concern never alluded to in any discussion of mandatory maternity leave). Only one woman articulated unambiguous support for men's paid or unpaid leave from employment during or immediately after the birth of a child. Equal parenting, it seemed, starts during a child's toddler years. For infants, the mother remained the parent who mattered.

⬚ Summary and Conclusions

At Bay Chapel and Mount Olive, the institutional practices, the sermons, the texts in the bookstore, even the architecture that housed congregational life establishes environments where highly differentiated gender roles receive positive social sanctions. This phenomenon is not limited to these two churches but appears to hold true for Christian fundamentalist congregations in general (DeBerg 1990; Bendroth 1993). The differentiated gender roles Bay Chapel and Mount Olive proffer to women exclude them from most positions of authority and associate them with family and home life in a distinctive, and restrictive, way. In the process, they elicit women's complicity in female/male heterosexuality complementarities dominated by men.

From a feminist viewpoint, the interpretation of gender that congregational practices promote is problematic. It bars equal relations between the sexes at the doors of home and church. In the home, submission (albeit, at its most positive, mutual) is expected to reign. In the church, males dominate authority, and women attempt to compensate for this through female power coalitions. Interpretations of gender predicated upon separate-sphere socialization for women and men have, in the culture at large, proven detrimental to women. For instance, female-dominated childrearing appears a primary causal factor in cultural misogyny (Dinnerstein 1976). Separate-sphere socialization masks women's important economic contributions to culture and permits their material exploitation by men (Segal 1987). Within nuclear families, separate-sphere ideology results in women receiving less justice than men (Okin 1989).

At Bay Chapel and Mount Olive, the ideal order for family life offers diminished support for women's wage-earning work. Women are encouraged to focus their time and energy on home life. Congregational rhetoric supports women who earn wages because they have to, not because they want to. Yet male believers are also supported in disinvesting themselves from the workplace to concentrate their energies on home. Still men are unquestionably expected to work outside the home and are supported for doing so, while women who "have" to work outside the home are pitied. To the extent that female believers shape their lives in accord with this family order, their access to economic, social, and political resources that could empower them within their families and communities is circumscribed. This diminished empowerment places female believers at increased physical and economic risk. Research on domestic violence reveals the existence of an inverse relationship between wife battery and a woman's income: men batter female partners who do not bring money into the family economy more frequently than those who do (Frieze-Hanson and McHugh 1992; Okin 1989).

Still, any account of the gender and family order taught by Bay Chapel and Mount Olive that portrays it in totally bleak terms would be misleading. Similar to the findings of Stacey and Burdick, my research showed that individual women are drawing upon the religiously sponsored differentiated gender roles at Bay Chapel and Mount Olive to negotiate improvements in personal life (Stacey 1990; Burdick 1993). Through their involvement with their church, believing women are saving marriages they want to save, quitting jobs they want to quit, working when they want to work, and bearing or adopting children when they want to rear families.[8] They are accomplishing the goals they have set for themselves in their lives, and mining the gender resources of Bay Chapel and Mount Olive to assist them in the process—though, as Lesley's story disclosed, these same symbolic resources can also function to thwart, as well as fulfill, women's personal agendas.

Bay Chapel and Mount Olive authoritatively present themselves as communities of spiritual and emotional support for pregnant women—whether married or not. To the extent that they are effective in influencing congregational attitudes to look favorably upon pregnant women, this could bear significant results. According to recent research on religious factors and the emotional well-being of adolescent mothers, social support is a critical factor in the short- and long-term well-being of young women who give birth and their infants. Bay Chapel and Mount Olive may offer healthful alternative communities for pregnant unmarried women who opt for single parenting (Sorenson, Grindstaff, and Turner 1995).

Feminist-supported family reforms have permeated the thought of female believers at Bay Chapel and Mount Olive in ways many of them do not realize. Though most Bible-believing women say they are not feminists—insisting that their goal is to be godly women—they express unanimous support for equal pay for women and men and readily discuss wife battery as a serious societal problem. They favor passage of marital rape laws and talk poignantly about the importance of a father's involvement in childrearing. While women maintained that submission is their relational ideal in marriage, they commonly depict it as a tactical approach employed by both husband and wife to encourage more just interactions than their parents had. Tellingly, Amy insists that family order founded on mutual submission provides her with more intrafamilial power than her mother ever had.

> For my mother, if my father said "Jump," she jumped. If he said, "Make my dinner," she made his dinner. She did everything that he would ask her to do, even if it wasn't the right timing for her. She could have been in the garage and if he said, "Honey, get my coffee," she would go get his coffee—although he might be in the kitchen! To me, that wasn't right in a relationship. Submission in our life is much different. It's more of a sharing. We give to each other. There might be something I might have wanted to do, but I don't. So I give myself to my husband, so that we can enjoy something else that he might have liked. Then, another week, we do something I like. We give to each other in that way. If it's not a good timing for me, I'm able to come out and say, "No, I can't do that right now. You're going to have to do it yourself."

Like Amy, the other women of Bay Chapel and Mount Olive believe that they have improved their positions within the nuclear family compared to their mothers' roles. They are, they believe, making good progress. Thus, one should be cautious about applying any totalizing label that implies that they have been coopted into an uncritical unity with authoritative leaders' pronouncements. Congregational rhetoric and female believers' ideas both overlap and differ. Though some enclave women's values vary significantly from feminist ones, the use of terms such as "postfeminist" or "antifeminist" to describe the role of fundamentalist women in contemporary American identity politics misconstrues the complex sociopolitical positions that Mount Olive and Bay Chapel women espouse.

Epilogue

Being Female and Fundamentalist in the Third Millennium

*In difference is the irretrievable loss of the il-
lusion of the one.*
　　　　　　　—Donna Haraway, *Simians,*
　　　　　　　Cyborgs, and Women

As godly women-in-progress, the women of Bay Chapel and
Mount Olive help guide religious congregations that try to
function as utopian families for their adherents. They take
people in regardless of dress and demand nothing monetary as
the price of admission. California-hip, they baptize at the beach
and do Bible-rap in worship. They show movies for free and
even provide the popcorn. They hold low-cost spirituality retreats at Palm Beach and sponsor half-price luncheons featur-
ing celebrity speakers. To the youthful, often jazzily attired
seekers who come through their doors, they provide pastors
who are cool, fuzzily authoritarian parent figures, with-it enough
not to go ballistic when someone arrives at a meeting wearing
shredded blue jeans but stern enough to provide strict guidance

on how to live, backed up by teleological and ontological rationales that justify their stance. In a cultural period characterized by its uncertain stabilization of individuals, congregations like Bay Chapel and Mount Olive are secure, readily available stabilizers. Believers invest sufficient time, money, and energy in congregational life to keep the church's facilities open and active day in, day out, year after year.

Yet family is only one of many metaphors that can be used to describe the complex public roles of Bay Chapel and Mount Olive. Each is also a resource center, a library, an entertainment complex, and an educational enterprise. Amid the postmodern ethos of images, interactive texts, and multiple readers, Mount Olive and Bay Chapel acknowledge a single text whose meaning, leaders proclaim, is easily discernable. Amid an accelerating, frenzied conservative lament over late capitalism's steady erosion of the grand narratives of Western civilization (Lyotard and Thébaud 1985), Bay Chapel and Mount Olive are suffused with a single grand narrative, delivered with the tantalizing bonus that it is this narrative alone that makes sense of all human history. Amid a cultural milieu in which realness increasingly derives from reproduction (Baudrillard 1983), Mount Olive and Bay Chapel support the supreme meaningfulness of a unique, unrepeatable event. Bending neither to the secularized left nor to the magical right, these Christian fundamentalist congregations are narrowly religious. They are composed of people who believe in "some conception of a supernatural being, world, or force, and the notion that the supernatural is active, that events and conditions here on earth are influenced by the supernatural" (Stark and Bainbridge 1985, 5).

The services staged at Bay Chapel and Mount Olive are half soft-rock music, with excellent production values that rival secular entertainment. In fact, the skill of these new Christian fundamentalists in adapting modern cultural products is responsible for a great deal of the tension that exists between them and some old-line fundamentalists. It also stimulates considerable antagonism between them and dedicated secularists. If they had chosen to mark themselves as devout religious believers by adopting special clothing and withdrawing as much as possible from modern life, as the Hicksite Amish or the Lubavitchers do, they could have been tagged quaint and possibly mined as a cultural product by nonparticipants (Adorno 1994). But contemporary Christian fundamentalists increasingly are culturally aggressive. Reprising a quintessential American can-do attitude, Bay Chapel and Mount Olive participate in a contemporary Christian movement struggling to remain part of American culture while redefining it from within and thereby to redefine modernity itself, by converting its most seductive products (rock music, videos, commercial packaging) to Christian purposes (Hadden and Shupe 1988). As high-growth congregations, Bay Chapel and Mount Olive are committed to harnessing the seductive power of contemporary ephemera to further an alternative Christian counterculture. Thus, for those involved with them, it is easy to perceive the self as taking part in an imploded world building, recreating the self as a being-for-God. In this, these congregations exhibit a significant compatibility with the new paradigm described by Steven Warner (Warner 1993). Bay Chapel and Mount Olive are centers of achieved moral identity, a heady elixir that attracts people to spend themselves in the late twentieth-century American marketplace of religion.

To women attempting to make sense out of often very confused and confusing lives, the religious goods on display at Mount Olive or Bay Chapel can hold considerable appeal. They offer clear, if not always well argued, answers to persistent questions from which the secular media, diverting as they are, cannot finally distract human attention. Why are we alive? Is there any meaning to human existence? Why is there so much suffering and loss in the world? What happens when we die? These are questions that modern science has not and perhaps cannot answer. But they are the questions that Bay Chapel and Mount Olive specialize in addressing.

Surcharges and Bonuses for Women

Once they join Bay Chapel or Mount Olive, believers are imaginatively and concretely transported into a symbolic world where gender is a highly salient category of human identity. It determines which meetings they can attend, what offices they can hold, and how they are expected to relate to their God. In daily life, it guides interfamilial relations. As the details of congregational gendering are explored, it becomes evident that the religious goods that Mount Olive and Bay Chapel offer levy a surcharge on women. The most notable of these gendered expenses comes in the area of religious authority. At both churches, men govern the patterns of congregational life. If male domination of congregational authority detracts from women's enjoyment of their congregation's religious goods, but they do not want to abandon their religious family, they must take refuge in its female subrealm, the all-female that accommodate the pressure of fundamentalist women's changing needs while allowing the congregation to present itself as a strict, intransigent institution that offers an alternative to cultural norms (Iannaccone 1990).

Yet each congregation offers bonuses to women as well, at any rate to heterosexual, married women. In overall congregational life, male responsibility is emphasized. Marriage is valued, and sexual fidelity within marriage is demanded. Male involvement in parenting is expected. Frances Fitzgerald has argued that women might have invented such churches, given their prohibition of "traditional male vices" and positive sanctions for male commitment to family life. Given the economic needs and disparities that married women with children face, "To tell 'Dad' that he made all the decisions might be a small price to pay to get the father of your children to become a respectable middle-class citizen" (Fitzgerald [1981] 1986).

The other bonuses women enjoy at Mount Olive and Bay Chapel are located in women's ministries and the female social networks they support. The all-female enclaves specifically nurture the spiritual development of women and are resources of thick emotionality that women can access as needed to support their daily lives. In women's retreats and Bible studies, women exercise major symbolic power. They teach, preach (although they do not call it that), and preside over sacramental rituals. Were it not for the tradition within sociological analysis of focusing on overall group leadership and organizational independence as key variables, the women's ministry programs at Bay Chapel and Mount Olive would, by number of participants and hours invested per week, qualify as sizable churches in their own right. In the enclave context, women at times administer the sacraments of communion and baptism, which means that here at least they are exercising the full range of Christian ecclesial office—a rare phenomenon in Christendom, even at the cusp of the third millennium. That women lead only when men are not present nuances the symbolic import of their leadership, but it does not negate it.

Traditionalism and Women

It is important to keep in mind that the teachings about women, men, and family life that are part of the sacred canopy covering Bay Chapel and Mount Olive are not new even though the late twentieth-century American audience listening to them is. Given that religious communities generally function to conserve values within cultures, they tend to be harbors of tradition; yet the congregations upon which my analysis is based are less than forty years old and roughly 50 percent of their membership is female (with women ages twenty-one to forty-one being the largest group). While respect for the richness of tradition or generationally ingrained religious habits might account for women's participation in certain religious communities, it cannot be considered an important factor in their participation in Mount Olive or Bay Chapel. Instead, they must be acknowledged as ascriptive believers (Warner 1993). Women affiliate with Bay Chapel and Mount Olive because they choose them, not necessarily because they are continuing in or returning to a traditional religious practice of their youth.

Rational Choice and Female Fundamentalists

Originally developed in the field of economics, "rational choice" is a scientific theory of human behavior. It posits that human beings possess stable sets of preferences that they invariably attempt to maximize, subject to the constraints of the market. When used as an interpretive tool to understand religious behavior, rational choice theory assumes that "individuals act rationally, weighing the costs and benefits of potential actions . . . choosing the actions that maximize their net benefits" (Iannaccone 1995, 2). When speaking about their motives for involvement in Christian fundamentalism, the language of the women I interviewed resonated with rational choice ideas. It offends female believers to think that people who do not share their religious beliefs might attribute their involvement in Christian fundamentalism to their being overwhelmed by the ideas and desires of men. At Mount Olive, Louise bluntly declared, "We have very good reasons for the choices we made. We are not just airheads who say to men, 'Oh, is that what I should do? Okay!' We have each thought about it and made choices. We have had to fight this through and figure out who we are and where we are."

To the extent that rational choice theory holds viable explanatory power regarding women's involvement in Christian fundamentalism, it suggests that Elaine, Mary, and the other women of Mount Olive and Bay Chapel engage in a social calculus whose results favor their involvement in a highly gender-restrictive faith. The question rational choice theory forces to the fore is, What do women gain through their involvement in this particular form of religiosity? What, if anything, do Elaine and Mary and Janet want that their faith's sacred canopy, with its sacred gender partition, provides? The price women pay for their involvement is readily evident. But what benefits do they accrue?

One critical benefit, according to my respondents, is consistency. At a time when American cultural scripts for women are increasingly in conflict with the lived reality of women's lives (Willard 1988), Mount Olive and Bay Chapel women are constructing and managing socioreligious networks that trespass boundaries between religion and private life, religion and social policy, religion and the state, while affirming the boundaries between themselves and men. Believing that the public sphere can support, reinforce, confuse, or neglect moral choices, the enclaves are small-scale social movements in which women work together to push their way out of modernity's boxes to achieve moral consonance among home, school, employment, and the state. Grounding their personal identity in faith, they embrace constancy and refuse to transform themselves from worldview to worldview depending upon their institutional environment of the moment, as good moderns are expected to do.

These findings are in considerable accord with those of Judith Stacey in her landmark research work on modern American families. Discovering a high level of participation in gender-restrictive religion by the women in her study, Stacey investigated the phenomenon and determined that for some young women "more exhausted than outraged" (Stacey 1990,

138), fundamentalist congregations were attractive because they offered "a flexible resource for reconstituting gender and kinship relationships" (Stacey 1990, 139). According to Stacey, the reduced economic opportunities of a postindustrial economy were forcing American women into painful personal and professional compromises in order to sustain familial intimacy and "to cope with family crises" (Stacey 1990, 263). Her conclusion was that contemporary women were attracted to fundamentalist congregations because in these groups they find support for their compromised positions.

Facing a myriad of unresolved conflicts among the quintuple roles of wife, mother, wage earner, housekeeper, and citizen, Bay Chapel and Mount Olive women are opting for involvement in religious communities that support them in the role of believer, which relativizes all other demands upon the self. Before anything else, Bay Chapel and Mount Olive women are people of faith, committed to furthering their relationship with their God. To see if rational choice theory is helpful in evaluating their involvement in these congregations, it is critical to determine the extent to which their option for a unified identity is a positive rational move given their particular sociocultural environment. For Bay Chapel and Mount Olive women, the environment in question is a postindustrial United States in which significant social meaning is achieved through work but workplaces do not deal with the female body as normative. It is a nation whose public rhetoric insists that family values are paramount but that offers a social environment where parenting largely remains the responsibility of women, where commitments to parenting are not valued, where education is absurdly underfunded and child care grossly inadequate. It is a country that lauds mobility, flexibility, and pragmatism as highly desirable traits and whose institutions generate personal worlds of isolation, disruption, and detachment for those associated with them. Given that most Bay

Chapel and Mount Olive women are married and engaged in parenting young children, their involvement in Christian fundamentalism can be interpreted not only as a quest for faith but also as a move to obtain cosmological backing for the commitment of male partners to the women's and their children's well-being at a period of maximum economic and social vulnerability.

A major objection to embracing rational choice theory to interpret contemporary women's involvement in Christian fundamentalism has to do with the loss of power women experience in the movement. Yet to Bay Chapel and Mount Olive women, there is no significant dissonance between the distribution of authority and power in congregational life and that of public life elsewhere. And as earlier chapters reveal, fundamentalist women can and do exercise considerable power in the religious institutions they join, in spite of their exclusion from official positions of authority.

Another consideration is the devaluation of women that is seemingly woven into the sacred canopy of Christian fundamentalism. How can it be a rational choice for women to get involved with a group that privileges men and thereby supports the notion of female inferiority?

Yet Mount Olive and Bay Chapel women split these issues in two. While acknowledging congregational authority as the province of men, they generally do not believe that the domination of religious authority by men is attributable to any superior qualities that men alone possess. An important cohort difference arose among women over this, however. Older fundamentalist women (thirty-one and up) attribute men's dominance of authority to "the order of God" and describe it as extending to all aspects of public life. To these women, communal leadership is not an honor; it is a responsibility assigned by God to men, a burden that men have to shoulder in human communities of all sorts. Young fundamentalist women (between twenty-one and thirty) differ. Unlike their senior sisters, young fundamentalists make a clear distinction between congregations and other communities. To them religious congregations are special sites, where different rules apply. Willing to accede authority to men in the congregation (though at times reluctantly so), younger fundamentalist women claim that any privileged male claim to authority stops at the far side of the church doors. This difference between younger and older believing women over how far the sacred gender wall extends became most obvious in the cohort differences that arose over whether they would support a female candidate for president. Younger female believers unanimously claim that they would; older ones were either ambivalent or opposed. Thus, although younger female believers employ much of the same gender language as older ones, they appear to interpret that language in a different, more egalitarian way.

The role of institutional rhetoric also must be considered in evaluating the usefulness of rational choice theory for understanding women's faith choices. Bay Chapel and Mount Olive have an aggressive stance toward congregational growth. As new congregations requiring growth to survive, they are specially designed to attract new adult believers. Congregational practices, programs, rituals, and classes are all fashioned to be inviting to newcomers. Given this, it would be surprising if many women experiencing acute life crises did not end up in the fold. With scant energy to expend evaluating alternatives, women are likely to favor religious alternatives that offer readily accessible, easily grasped answers. Mount Olive, Bay Chapel, and similar high-growth contemporary Christian fundamentalist congregations respond adroitly and with well-honed skill to such needs.

Thus, rational choice theory does offer some useful insights into women's attraction to and involvement in Christian fundamentalism. Yet for all of the theory's explanatory appeal, I cannot condone the categorization of fundamentalist women as rational choosers, primarily because rational choice theory to me implies a cool, middle-class sensibility. It posits a motivation dynamic in which one explores and compares the available options and then selects the one most advantageous to oneself. Such calculation stands in stark contrast to the experiences of Bay Chapel and Mount Olive women, who were rarely if ever cool when they made decisions of faith. As Cathy's conversion story in chapter 2 illustrates, the women who joined Mount Olive and Bay Chapel most often did so in the midst of incredible life chaos. The conversion experience tends to be very hot and very emotional; yet this does not necessarily preclude the presence of calculation. Further, to describe a woman's affiliation with Bay Chapel or Mount Olive as a rational choice implies that she joined after considering meaningful alternatives. Given the widespread sexism that marks most religious groups in the United States, meaningful alternatives for women are slim. If a woman's decision to join a Christian fundamentalist congregation is a rational one in terms of rational choice theory—which, to a limited extent, it may be— evidence indicates that such rationality must be attributable to an egregiously gender-biased context and often is achieved accidentally rather than by design.

Political Implications of Women's Involvement with Second-Wave Christian Fundamentalism

While the debate in the United States over personal and public conceptions of women and men is far from new, major political and economic changes in American life mark its recent progress. Sexual harassment laws signal the public's increasing willingness to marshal political clout to establish legal restrictions on unwelcome sexual overtures in the workplace. Conversely, the dearth of punitive action that followed the public exposure of the Tailhook scandal discloses the limits of that clout. As this debate increasingly entails legal and economic consequences, political dynamics are an integral aspect of their resolution, reflexively shaping the arguments themselves. Thus, the form this quarrel takes depends to a large extent on who is on what side of an issue, or, to put it in more postmodernish terms, who can be made to appear to be on what side. Mothers Against Drunk Driving is an example of a masterly social-movement initiative in this regard. The organizational name prescriptively casts opponents in a harsh light ("drunk drivers") and claims a parental, emotional stake in the issue ("mothers"). Both terms problematize the possibility of opposition. Who can, without incurring considerable discomfort, opt to be against mothers and for driving drunks? The MADD image shapes the issue and the combatants within it in favor of good old mom. Rhodes points to the image bind Hillary Clinton has experienced as First Lady as one of "feminine versus feminist . . . a double bind confronting women." When women's issues are framed in this way (a typical Western dualism), if one allows oneself to be shaped by either frame, the result will "alienat[e] a substantial portion of the population" (Rhode 1995, 699).

Since women make up the largest population group in this country, the extent to which women unite on issues, or at least sustain the appearance of substantial unity on them, translates into a formidable political power influencing their outcome. Not surprisingly, significant attempts have been made to split the appearance, if not the reality, of women's solidarity on issues. Postmodernity's multivocality is at best ambiguous in this regard. Individual women may have good reason to disclaim solidarity with all women; however, it is only by working together to address social and economic circumstances detrimental to women that women can wield the political force necessary to improve their own lives. Fragmentation of women's voices blunts women's ability to dictate political resolutions favorable to them.

Two vivid female images floated out into American culture that fragment the political unification of women are the Christian fundamentalist and the feminist. The former, so the popular culture narrative goes, is a homemaker who submits to her pastor at church and her husband at home and considers feminism anathema. The latter is an embittered working woman who hates men, submits to no one, and considers God and domestic life anathema. In public policy debates, these two images are trotted out to remind voters that not all women agree on the issue at hand. A vote for one position can be read as a vote against the other. Because most conservative Protestant women do disagree with the majority feminist position on abortion, they have been culturally read as antifeminists (Himmelstein 1986; Dworkin 1983) or as postfeminists who have embraced conservative Christianity because the women's movement putatively has failed them in some regard (Stacey 1990).

In a review of feminist research in the sociology of religion, Mary Jo Neitz provided some insight into how the academic literature may have been a factor in the political polarization of fundamentalist women and feminists (Neitz 1993). When the initial surge of academic interest in Christian fundamentalism came in the 1970s, three concerns dominated research: the public writings of male leaders, fundamentalism's influence on American politics, and the relevance of fundamentalism's growth to mainline liberal Protestantism. Early feminist analyses explored the political role fundamentalist parachurch organizations such as Jerry Falwell's Moral Majority played in debates over the Equal Rights Amendment and abortion. Thus, in the first surge of academic interest in fundamentalism, little serious attention was paid to fundamentalist women. According to Neitz. One early study of women's participation was so unsympathetic toward the women involved that it "fails to foster an understanding of their world views" (Neitz 1993, 171).

In my work at Bay Chapel and Mount Olive, I encountered

a few women who articulated anti- and postfeminist positions but several, including the leader of women's ministries at Mount Olive, told me they consider themselves to be feminists. While many believing women hold positions on certain issues that contradict widely held feminist ones—most notably, on abortion—Mount Olive and Bay Chapel women also display overwhelming support for feminist economic and political reforms such as the institution of marital rape laws. Belying the image of conservative female believers as a seamlessly united political front, women maintain positions on various issues that range from pro- to non- to antifeminist, depending upon whom you ask about what.

This microanalytical study of women's ministries at Bay Chapel and Mount Olive focused on the interaction of individual women with particular Christian institutions and provides a glimpse into the complexity of the issues raised by women's participation in second-wave fundamentalist Christianity. This very complexity, the messiness of social experience, may explain why, more than twenty-five years after Mary Daly first published *The Church and the Second Sex*, Christian institutions are not the egalitarian organizations Daly initially believed they could so easily be (Daly 1968). Microanalysis at the congregational level at Bay Chapel and Mount Olive reveals a sexist congregational ideology—more sexist than would be found in liberal, moderate, or even most evangelical Protestant congregations. However, the assault upon women that results is not a totalizing one. The women of Bay Chapel and Mount Olive do not consider themselves to be introjecting a message of inferiority by their involvement in these congregations. They also do not perceive their congregations as spiritually handicapping them. The women who joined these churches almost always did so for reasons other than the actualization of their leadership potential. Many came to these congregations incredibly wounded, needing succor to survive. Whether they were going to be fully realized as persons or accorded equal rights with men were not important issues to the women I interviewed.

With this in mind, I encourage those who study and write about fundamentalist influences on the American political scene, rather than focusing almost exclusively on male pastors, to also approach female believers as a critical source of information on these movements. To award the public voice of North American Protestant fundamentalism to an elite pastoral minority is a mistake. It ignores the reality that at least half the participants within it are women who, due to the overdetermination of their religious experience by gender in congregational life, develop distinct ideas and experiences about the meaning of fundamentalist faith. In addition, since the exercise of authority and power within congregational life is at times in conflict with the movement's dominant teaching on sex roles, these teachings should be considered a rhetorical effort to sway the behavior of highly independent, diverse congregations rather than a description of or prescription for authority and power patterns in congregational life.

Summary and Conclusions

It is a sign of remarkable cultural change that fundamentalist Christianity, following the trajectory of blue jeans and rock music, has become a countercultural youth movement. Yet like those two artifacts of popular culture, it has been changed in the process. Where first-wave fundamentalist Christians wailed about end times, second-wave fundamentalist Christians celebrate them (Hadden and Shupe 1988). Where initially fundamentalist countercultural tropes attracted those who rejected modern life and tried to hold it at bay, second-wave fundamentalists actively attempt to reshape modernity by turning its products to their advantage. One of the most perceptive feminists in religion studies, Elisabeth Schussler-Fiorenza, described the challenge of feminist hermeneutics in religion as being one that takes seriously the sociohistorical situation of women. She challenges feminist scholars to take seriously how and why women become Christian in particular places and times (Schussler-Fiorenza 1990).

In my study of the women at Bay Chapel and Mount Olive, I have attempted to do just that, and I learned many things in the process. Taking seriously the historical context of their decisions, I came to recognize how the women of Bay Chapel and Mount Olive struggled to achieve integrity in their faith and exercise power and authority in their congregations and homes. But I retain significant reservations about the way they do so. I remain unconvinced that Christianity is a religion whose ideals center on the nuclear family or dual-sphere gender roles. Liberal Christian that I am, I am still persuaded that Christianity is a religion whose cardinal value is practiced love, which reveals itself in dedicated work for justice and freedom, and in providing clothing, food, and shelter to those who lack them. While I understand the pragmatic compromises many of the women I came to know during this study made, I do not believe they are the best long-term strategies for women.

In spite of the image they present of being an upscale, ideal family, Bay Chapel and Mount Olive congregations are not viable ideals of family life even for those who agree with their viewpoint. Each is a megacongregation, with thousands of adherents and sizable caches of material resources to draw upon. Such sizable institutions bear little resemblance to the actual families involved with them, in which rearing and nurturing of family members occur amidst profound constraints on time, energy, and financial resources. Real families take time, money, investment of self. They limit as much as support individuality. Family life requires hard work; yet the type of work it demands is structurally devalued in contemporary American life by dis-advantaging, both in material prosperity and in status, those who pursue it.

As I conclude this story of the women of Mount Olive and Bay Chapel, the goals that inspired me to begin this research reconverge amid the lines of text like beckoning clouds. At the closing focus meeting with the Mount Olive women, Mary startled me when she made the following comment at the end of the meeting: "We are going from glory to glory and strength to strength. You make mistakes, and you learn from the mistakes and you move on. We are evolving constantly. We should be growing. We are called to go forward and not stay in the same place. So I'll bet if you did interview us again, we'd have differ-ent answers because we are changing all the time."

That Christian fundamentalist women such as Mary consider change an integral aspect of their religious identity—something my findings both confirm and deny—may be a key source of the hope that keeps them involved in the religious groups. It indicates that the appeal second-wave fundamentalist Christian-ity has for women is more multifaceted and, from a liberal per-spective, more ambiguous than is often perceived. While the pain and struggle disclosed in women's conversion narratives go far toward explaining why some women are initially attracted to these groups, once they get involved and discover the un-equal lot that their religious community assigns to them, why do they stay? The disempowerment a woman encounters in a Christian fundamentalist congregation is easy to document and should not be underemphasized. But the empowerment she may discover or build there, though not always immediately obvious, must be acknowledged as well.

⬡ *Coda*

The years I spent studying Christian fundamentalist congregations were personally challenging. A liberal Christian, I began the study believing I would have little in common with the conservative believers I would meet, whose outlook I imagined to be profoundly dissonant with my own. A committed feminist, I considered it likely that the women and men I would be interviewing were my key political and social antagonists in what for me is one of the central commitments of my life: the ongoing battle against sexism. As I have reflected on the time I spent involved in the faith lives of these two communities—not only interviewing female fundamentalists but studying biblical texts with them, worshiping in their sanctuaries, going on retreats with them in the country, sharing meals in their homes, listening to their stories, and eventually telling some of my own—I realized that I had undertaken one of the most amazing adventures possible—that of getting to know an "other" quite different from yet related to myself.

By the project's end, I realized that while I disagreed with many of their cardinal ideas, I had grown to admire the faith and faithfulness of the women of Bay Chapel and Mount Olive. I have rarely encountered a Christian preacher, female or male, whose passionate, mystical speaking presence fascinated me as much as Elaine's did, even though some of the ideas she espoused seemed irrational, and some of the positions she held were quite contrary to my own. In fact, I consider it a poignant paradox that some of the most impassioned public speeches on the Christian faith I have ever heard were delivered not by female or male clergy nurtured in the bastions of Christian liberalism out of which I come, but by the uncredentialed laywomen of Mount Olive and Bay Chapel, who refuse to call what they do preaching.

SCHEDULE OF INTERVIEWEES

Bay Chapel

Ellen	Women's pastor
Ann	Wednesday morning leader
Beth	Wednesday morning leader
Cathy	Wednesday morning participant
Dorothy	Wednesday morning leader
Amy	Tuesday morning participant
Adele	Wednesday morning participant
Rachel	Thursday night participant
Kiersten	Thursday night participant
Caryn	Tuesday morning leader; staff aerobics instructor
Cicely	Wednesday morning participant
Teresa	Monday night single women's study leader; general staff assistant
Roxanne	Thursday night participant
Judith	Thursday night study leader; staff receptionist
Sonia	Tuesday morning participant
Silvia	Tuesday morning participant

Barbara	Monday night leader
Nan	Tuesday morning leader
Lesley	Monday night leader
Linda	Monday night leader
Jane	Thursday night leader
Joan	Tuesday morning participant
Margot	Monday night participant
Nancy	Monday night leader; member of worship team

Mount Olive

Elaine	Head of women's ministries; senior pastor's wife
Martha	Bible study leader
Jenny	Bible study participant
Vicky	Bible study participant
Cheryl	Bible study participant
Darla	Bible study participant; attends Calvary Costa Mesa
Sally	Bible study participant
Cory	Bible study participant
Maria	Bible study leader
Irene	Bible study leader
Molly	Bible study leader; secretary to senior pastor; pastor's wife
Leslie	Bible study participant; daughter of Elaine
Nicole	Bible study leader
Dona	Bible study participant
Julie	Bible study leader; manager of independent study programs; pastor's wife
Sandra	Bible study leader
Mary	Bible study leader; administrative assistant to Elaine
Louise	Bible study leader; pastor's wife
Paula	Bible study participant

Beth   Bible study participant
Josie   Bible study leader
Hope   Bible study leader
Joyce   Bible study leader; pastor's wife
Terri   Bible study participant

APPENDIX B

INTERVIEW GUIDE

1. *Personal Life*

Tell me a little bit about who you are . . .

> your name
> age
> education
> hometown
> ethnic background
> work history

What kind of music did you like growing up? What do you like now?

What movie that you saw in the past year did you like best and why?

What is your favorite TV program? Why do you like it?

Do you have any hobbies?

> [If yes] What are they and how much time per week do you spend on them?
> [If no] Why not?

How often and how far have you moved in the last twenty years?

What do you like most about your current way of life? What do you like the least about it?

Are there changes in your life that you would like to make now? What keeps you from making them?

2. Relationships with Men

Are you now married or single?

Have you ever been married before? Describe.

[If now single] Are you currently involved in a serious relationship with someone?

> [If yes]
>> Please sketch for me an outline of that relationship including how and where you met, highs, lows, separations, reconciliations.
>> Does submission play a role in that relationship? How? Why/why not?

> [If no, probe.]

[If now married]

> Please sketch for me an outline of your marital history, including how you and your spouse met, highs, lows, separations, reconciliations.

> Were you married when you started coming to Mount Olive/Bay Chapel?

> [If yes] What was going on in your relationship at that time?

> [If no] Were you romantically involved with anyone?

>> [If yes] What was happening with that relationship when you began attending Mt Olive/Bay Chapel?

How important is marriage in your life? Why?

[If married] how does your marriage function?

> How many hours a week do you and your husband spend alone together?

> How much, by percentage, does each of you contribute to the family income?

> Who plans family activities?

Who literally pays the bills?

Who does the cooking?

Who washes the clothes?

[If there are children] Who does what with the children?

How are major family decisions made, such as moving, or
buying a car?

Submission

Tell me a little about submission in marriage. First, what is it?

Does it vary from person to person?

[If no comment is made on them, ask about wife's and husband's
roles.]

[If single] Will you follow the practice of submission when
married?

[If yes] Why?

[If no] Why not?

[If married]

Do you and your husband follow this practice? If so, could
you tell me a little about how you see submission shaping interactions between you and your husband?

If you wanted to go visit your mother (assuming she's living), and your husband told you that you could not go,
what would you do?

Does the practice of submission apply to your sex lives?

[If yes] How does that work?

[If no] Why not?

Does submission make your marriage different from the
marriages of people who do not practice it?

[If yes] In what way?

[If no] Why not?

Are there areas of your relationship where submission has
not been helpful? Describe.

Are there ways in which you would not submit to your
husband?

[If yes] Please describe them.

[If no] Why not?

How did you learn about the practice of submission?

General

Not necessarily thinking of your own marriage but marriage in general, are there times when a couple should divorce?

[If yes] Under what circumstances?

[If no] Why not?

Again, not necessarily thinking of your own marriage but marriage in general, is it possible for a husband to rape his wife?

[If no] Why not?

[If yes] What do you think should be done about it? [Probe: Should there be legal recourse for the wife?]

One pastor—from the pulpit—said that a woman should not have to live with a physically abusive spouse, and if any woman in the congregation was being abused, he personally would go to her house and help her pack up and leave. Do you think this is something a pastor should say from the pulpit? Why or why not?

3. Relationships with Children/Family

Describe your family for me. Who do you think of as your family? Of how many people does it consist?

If we were taking a long bus trip together, and I asked you to tell me about your family, what would you say?

What is important in parenting children today?

[If there are children]

Where do your children go to school? How was this decision made?

How did you learn to parent your children?

Should children who break parental rules be physically punished?

How much time per week do you spend with each family
member?

Does your faith affect the way you parent a lot, a moderate amount, very little, or not at all? How does it do
this?

4. *Philosophical Questions about Women and Men*

In what ways are women and men the same?

In what ways are women and men different?

How do you know this?

Are these similarities and differences the same everywhere in
the world?

    [If yes] Why?

    [If no] Why not?

Do these ever change in history?

    [If yes] What would be a good example of this?

    [If no] Why not?

Are there separate roles for women and men

    in the home?

        [If no] Why not?

        [If yes] What are they?

    in parenting?

        [If no] Why not?

        [If yes] What are they?

    in church? [Probe: pastor? council member? usher?]

        [If no] Why not?

        [If yes] What are they?

    in education?

        [If no] Why not?

        [If yes] What are they?

    in the workplace?

        [If no] Why not?

        [If yes] What are they?

in government?

> [If no] Why not?

> [If yes] What are they?

Some writers in the women's movement have said that women, through mothering, develop a special way of connecting to others that influences the way they decide what's right and wrong. They call this way of deciding moral issues an "ethic of care." They then contrast this to men's way of deciding right from wrong, which they call an ethic of justice or rules. Do you agree with this idea? Why or why not?

Other writers in the women's movement have said that until women have financial equality with men, women will be oppressed by men. Do you agree with this idea? Why or why not?

5. *On Affiliating with Mount Olive/Bay Chapel*

Tell me a little about your religious history.

What religious influences did you have growing up?

Have you ever been involved with another Christian group?

> [If yes] Who/what/when?

> [If no] Why not?

Have you had a conversion experience?

> [If yes] What was it like?

> [If no] Why do you think this has not occurred?

When did you first visit Mount Olive/Bay Chapel?

> What do you remember about that first visit?

> What was going on in your life at that time?

As you got involved with Mount Olive/Bay Chapel, was it a struggle or easy for you?

Did you get involved suddenly or gradually?

As you got involved with Mount Olive/Bay Chapel, how did your husband/family/friends respond?

Did your friendships change? Why/why not?

Did you have to make any changes in your life when you got
  involved with Mount Olive/Bay Chapel?
  [If yes] Could you describe a few of these for me?
  [If no] Why not?
Were there people who were role models for you when you first
  got involved with Mount Olive/Bay Chapel? Please describe
  them.
Was there a book, television show, radio program, or other that
  influenced you to get involved with [Mount Olive/Bay
  Chapel]?
How many of your family members and friends have gotten in-
  volved with Mount Olive/Bay Chapel since you did?
Right now, what events or activities at Mount Olive/Bay Chapel
  do you regularly attend?
How many hours per week are you typically involved at Mount
  Olive/Bay Chapel? [Probe for enclave activities versus
  mixed-sex events.]
Are you involved with any other religious groups in addition
  to Mount Olive/Bay Chapel? Describe.
What positions do you currently hold at Mount Olive/Bay
  Chapel?

6. *Practices and Experiences of Faith*

How often do you listen to Christian radio? Christian televi-
  sion? Which program/s, if any, do you regularly follow?
How often do you purchase or rent Christian cassette tapes or
  videos?
How many Christian books do you buy in a month?
Who is your favorite Christian author?
What version of the Bible do you prefer and why? How often
  do you read the Bible in a normal week?
When do you pray privately? When do you pray as a family?
What kinds of things do you pray for or about privately/as a
  family?

Have you ever had prayer answered? If so, tell me a little about one of the more memorable prayer responses you've had.

Do you call yourself a born-again Christian?

> [If yes] What does that mean?
>
> [If no] Why not?

Have you ever had what some might call a "religious experience"?

> [If yes] What form did it take?
>
> [If no] Why not?

What does God look like?

How does God work in the world? How do you know this?

When I've been involved in public prayer at Mount Olive/Bay Chapel events, I've heard God most often addressed as "father." How would you respond if you heard God addressed as "mother" during public prayer? Why?

Has God ever spoken to you in a dream? While you were awake? Please describe this.

Can you tell me what the spiritual realm is like?

What is a soul?

Does God treat women differently from men?

> [If yes] How/why?
>
> [If no] Why not?

Does your relationship with God affect your life? How?

Do you consider yourself a Protestant [as compared to a Roman Catholic or Greek Orthodox for instance]?

> [If yes] What does being a Protestant mean to you?
>
> [If no] Why not?

What do you think of Christians who are not involved with Mount Olive/Bay Chapel?

What do you think of those who are not Christian at all?

7. *Political World/Women's Political Issues*

Did you vote in the last presidential election?

What was the most important issue in that race?

Which candidate addressed it best? Why?

What do you think should be done to address it?

Would you vote for a female candidate for president? Why/why not?

Considerable media attention has been paid to the role of Christian values in government.

What are Christian values?

What role, if any, should they have in government?

Are you involved with a Christian political action group?

[If yes] Which one/s and why? [Probe: e.g., Christian Coalition, Focus on the Family]

[If no] Why not?

Has the women's movement of the last twenty years had any impact on you? Please elaborate.

What did you think of the ERA? Did you get involved, either for or against this movement? If so, how?

Would you describe yourself as a feminist? As a Christian feminist? Why/why not?

Sexual harassment was brought to national attention during the Clarence Thomas/Anita Hill confrontation in the Senate.

Did you watch or listen to any of the hearings?

Were the Hill/Thomas hearings discussed at any women's only event at Mount Olive/Bay Chapel? Please describe.

Has sexual harassment ever been addressed at Bay Chapel/Mount Olive in any way?

[If yes] How? Do you think the Hill/Thomas hearings influenced this?

[If no] Why not?

Do you think sexual harassment is a topic that should be addressed in congregational life? Why/why not?

Why is there so much controversy over abortion today? Have you been involved in this issue in any way? Describe.

In the past several decades, American women have entered the work force in increasing numbers. What do you think about this cultural change?

Some argue that in order truly to support the family, employers should be legally required to grant paid maternity and paternity leave to employees expecting or adopting a newborn baby. Do you agree with this idea? Why/why not?

Annual governmental reports indicate that women are paid less than men in every occupation. Assuming that these reports are accurate, what do you think of this pay difference?

Recently it was revealed that the federal government has spent a substantially larger amount of money researching diseases that primarily affect men than they have spent researching diseases that primarily affect women. Assuming health needs of women and men are about the same, what do you think of this spending ratio?

Are women's economic or political or health issues discussed in women-only events at Mount Olive/Bay Chapel?
[If yes] What is discussed?
[If no] Why not?

Since you started attending Mount Olive/Bay Chapel, have your political opinions changed?
[If yes] How?
[If no] Why not?

What are the most important issues confronting Christian women today?

8. *Women and the Enclaves*

When and why did you get involved with the all-female Bible study at Mount Olive/Bay Chapel?

[If Bay Chapel] Which women's study/ies do you now attend? Why did you pick this/these particular one/s?

How regularly do you attend the study?

How many hours a week do you spend, on the average, preparing for the Bible study sessions?

What do you do with your study notes when the sessions are over?

What do you like best about the women's Bible study?

What do you like the least about it?

If males were present, would the women's Bible study change?
 [If yes] Why? How?
 [If no] Why not?

In what other women-only activities at Mount Olive/Bay Chapel do you participate?

How many of your closest female friends are also involved with the women's ministries at Mount Olive/Bay Chapel?

Has your involvement in all-female faith groups affected your understanding of yourself as a woman?
 [If yes] How?
 [If no] Why not?

Has your involvement in all-female faith groups affected your faith life?
 [If yes] How?
 [If no] Why not?

Is there a woman or man in the Bible who serves as a role model/s for you?
 [If yes] Who/why?
 [If no] Why not?

What, if anything, is different between what you learn or experience in women's ministries and what you learn or experience in mixed-sex services, where women and men are both involved? What, if anything, is the same?

Who should lead women's ministry programs? Why?

Male ministers are paid. Should women who lead women's ministries also be paid? Why or why not?

Besides women's ministries at Mount Olive/Bay Chapel, are there other female-only activities in which you participate? Please describe them.

Are there any comments you would care to add?

NOTES 🏵

CHAPTER 1 *Inside a Christian Fundamentalist Congregation*

1. There is an ongoing discussion both in academic circles and within conservative Christianity over who is and is not a fundamentalist, partly due to a concern over whether fundamentalist is a pejorative term. I am one of a growing group of scholars involved in the scholarly study of fundamentalism who, rather than avoid the term fundamentalism, prefer to redefine it and make it more applicable to the diverse groups that now identify themselves as fundamentalists.

2. To support their definition, Richardson and David lump the Calvary Chapel movement in with the Children of God. This family grouping, while historically accurate and culturally defensible, is quite misleading in terms of congregational praxis. Calvary Chapel moral norms are conservative, in considerable contrast to COG, who used sex "as a recruitment tool" (Richardson and Davis 1983, 406).

3. Statistics are taken from congregational and pastoral leadership surveys developed and administered by the University of Southern California New Religious Movements research team led by Dr. Donald E. Miller in 1991–1992.

4. Roof and McKinney include Mormons, Jehovah's Witnesses, Christian Scientists, and Unitarian-Universalists in their category of "others" (Roof and McKinney 1987).

5. See Walter Rauschenbusch, *Theology of the Social Gospel* (New York: MacMillan, 1918) for a good introduction to Social Gospel beliefs.

6. Scopes lost in the local court; however, his conviction was later overturned on a technicality by the Tennessee Supreme Court (Mathisen 1982, 304).

CHAPTER 2 *Joining Up*

1. For an analysis of the value that reconfiguring biographical details to construct conversion narratives may have for converts, see Staples and

Mauss 1987. Staples and Mauss emphasize converts as active participants during the conversion process, who employ reconfigured biog-
raphies to assist them in their self-transformation.

2. For a succinct introduction to religious conversion stories in the United
States, see Holte 1992.

3. This is somewhat akin to the patristic concept of salvation as a sharing in divine life through union with Christ (Tillich [1967] 1968).

4. I define minimal involvement as attendance involving one to two religious events or activities a year.

5. By this, I am distancing myself slightly from Rambo's contention that
there is an underlying unity to all types of religious movement (Rambo
1993, 173). While sympathetic to the point he is making, I believe
there is a significant difference between what happens to an individual
who transfers from a typical Presbyterian to a typical United Method-
ist congregation and what happened to Bay Chapel and Mount Olive
women who were significantly nonreligious before their affiliation with
these groups. We may not be able to operationalize and test, with any
accuracy, for these differences—since not all human behavior is amenable to precise calculation—but this does not disprove their existence.

6. Steve Warner also employs conversion language to describe those af-
filiating with these particular groups. He aptly portrays the faith of believers as an "achieved religiosity" and states that because of it "these
are inherently churches of converts" (Warner 1993, 1076).

7. The three stages of women's conversion narratives aligned with
Rambo's seven-step conversion process as follows: (1) Preconversion
= Context, Crisis; (2) Salvation Event = Quest, Encounter, Interaction,
Commitment; (3) Postconversion = Consequences (Rambo 1993, 168–
169).

8. I define heavy religious involvement as regular attendance at more than
one religious activity or event each week.

9. This is fairly representative of the Roman Catholic population in southern California, which stands at 25 percent.

10. Given my limited population sample—one segment of a congregation-
based ministry at two different congregations—my results should not
be read as precluding the viability or likelihood of an instant, comprehensive, enduring conversion; however, they can be read, perhaps,
as indicative that a richer pool of descriptive lore exists for graduated
conversions. Additional research is required to ascertain the role that
congregations may be playing in supporting gradual versus instant conversion stories.

11. Other motivational factors cited were support for a husband's religious
preferences (4) and change in residence (3).

12. An ironic hermeneutic circle exacerbates this situation. The gender
bias that yields a social climate favorable to women's religious participation also encourages women to volunteer their labor rather than sell
it at market rates. The unpaid labor of women is a significant factor
in religious groups being able to offer free or low-cost services; yet the

high rate of women engaged in unpaid or poorly paid labor is what makes women the social group most in need of these services.

13. Further research would be required to operationalize and test either hypothesis. Following up on the role of economic factors in women's conversion stories would be a narrow, but theoretically rich, exploration, and I hope to see it done at some point in the near future.

14. My point here is to emphasize the tie between societal conditions and religious choices, not to imply either that these factors affect all women in an equivalent way or that men are somehow immune from their influence. The social organization of gender is globally diverse (Sanday 1981). Mount Olive and Bay Chapel adherents participate in that diversity.

CHAPTER 3 *The Hand That Rocks the Cradle*

1. See Rosaldo 1974 for illustrations of the usefulness of this distinction in the assessment of women's influence in traditional communities.

2. This exclusion is not absolute. Conservative Pentecostal congregations historically have been some of the most receptive to female leadership (Stark and Bainbridge 1985). Among the Calvary congregations in the United States, three have female senior pastors; however, this fact was never openly discussed at any intermovement meeting I attended.

3. Congregational surveys revealed no consistent pattern regarding which congregational positions of authority were reserved exclusively for males. In some congregations, it was solely the position of senior pastor. In some, the congregational board was considered an exclusively male province as well, while other congregations had marital couples on their boards.

4. It is important to note that my use of the word "preach" in connection with women leaders contradicts prevailing fundamentalist authoritative ideas, which insist that women can only teach or, at most, exhort. My dilemma over this choice of language has been acute. Fundamentalist women leaders stand in the pulpit and give biblically grounded lessons lasting thirty minutes or more to as many as two thousand women. This is behavior that, when males engage in it, is described as "preaching." Thus, to keep my work descriptively clear, I describe what the women were doing as preaching. Yet the use of different words by these groups to describe identical acts by women and men reveals much about the absoluteness of the gap between women and men inherent in their theological anthropology. When it comes to congregational life, fundamentalist ideas support a worldview in which the gender of the actor determines the nature of the act. Not very hidden in this worldview is a Durkheimian implication that being male is sacred. It is important to clarify the nonessential role of the audience's sex: males delivering a message to an all-female audience are still described as "preaching." Thus, in the dominant American

fundamentalist worldview, males must be speaking for "preaching" (a speech act with a connection to the transcendent) to occur. When females speak, regardless of where, or on what subject, or how long, their acts remain wholly tied to the profane; that is, women who engage in congregational speech acts do so solely out of their own learning.

5. Both congregations have high participant-to-staff ratios and provide a low level of staff support for most congregational programming. Yet women's groups suffer disproportionately in staff resource distribution because of a clash between movement staffing patterns and leadership norms. Practically all congregationally salaried pastors are male; yet women's programs must be led by women according to movement norms. Thus most enclave leadership is supplied by unpaid female volunteers.

6. This may be attributable to Bay Chapel's ongoing connection to a Pentecostal denomination that does ordain women into ministry.

7. Over the course of my study, it became obvious that a number of men in these congregations respected the talent of women in the movement. In taped interviews, several men expressed feelings of profound loss at not being able to study, or as they expressed it, "sit" under women they deemed especially knowledgeable. Their expressions of frustration relate to the dilemma of fundamentalist authority that Boone astutely diagnoses. Given the closed nature of fundamentalist discourse on authority, men as well as women can find themselves uncomfortably bound by its strictures. Still, in contrast to Boone's Foucauldian assertion that fundamentalist authority has no head, I found that men, more readily than women, could get around these strictures when they so desired (Boone 1989). For example, when Ann Graham Lotz (daughter of Ann and Billy Graham) was the keynote speaker at a Southern California Women in Leadership meeting at Riverside, California in 1993, a dozen men sat quietly among the eight hundred–plus women in attendance, taking avid notes. At Bay Chapel, a man who repeatedly requested it eventually gained admittance to a women's Bible study group. Female believers are not accorded these same boundary-crossing privileges.

8. Women married to senior pastors maintain diverse connections to the congregations their husbands lead. Some state that they are actively involved in leading congregational women due to a genuine interest in and commitment to women's ministries; others claim that they were forced into leadership either by their husband or by congregants. One reluctant women's leader asserted that she was not at all interested in congregational life but was unable to withdraw from the women's ministries, because the women in the congregation wouldn't let her: they expected her to lead them and demanded that she do so. This identity of "unwilling leader" that some senior pastors' wives describe may be partially attributable to a feminine rhetorical strategy. Under the congregation's theocratic, patriarchal governance scheme, positions of power are quite limited and largely deemed the province of males; thus,

women must deny any desire for power—thereby overtly submitting to the theocratic, patriarchal paradigm—before exercising it.

The problem this produces for a pastor's wife is acute. Ecclesial polity places her in a position of significant authority at the same time that theological anthropology makes her authoritatively distinct. This creates a condition where congregational women of necessity are forced to pressure a reluctant pastor's wife into involvement even if they might prefer not to, since under the rules of the game no other woman can serve as a comparable authoritative figure.

Among the pastors' wives I met, many were engaged in huge ministries among congregational women. One had twenty women working under her management. Another had been drawing in excess of two thousand women a week to Bible studies for years. Thus, the frequently maligned and often overlooked pastor's wife in many instances is a major source of religious life in a congregation.

9. For a very different, intriguing argument, see Ackerman's evocative contention that women's involvement in religious groups that officially marginalize them is an effort on their part to heighten their spirituality, and subsequently hone the use of their body as "the only alternative tactical weapon" available to them to achieve desired ends in family and societal conflict (Ackerman 1985, 76).

CHAPTER 4   *My Beloved Is All-Radiant*

1. The categorization of "religion" as something distinct from one's own enterprise is not a novel rhetorical ploy originating with Bay Chapel and Mount Olive. To attract believers, emergent religious groups must claim that events orchestrated by the group are distinct from the events of others. Often, the hermeneutical bridge such groups build to encourage new affiliation is double-anchored. The emergent group proclaims itself to be engaged in something novel, while simultaneously presenting itself as connected to an established religious tradition. By being both strange and familiar, the emergent group constructs a public image of itself as known and unknown: comfortable enough that potential believers can safely approach, intriguing enough that potential believers are lured into approaching, to discover if they have been missing something. For an ancient master of this dynamic pattern, see Paul's sermon on Mars Hill (Acts 17:22–32). Neoorthodox theologians, including Barth and Bruner, also emphasized relationship/religion distinctions, contrasting the ambiguity of human religion to the absoluteness of a living God.

2. In general outline, the definition of religious experience presented in this chapter follows that developed by Davis (1989). I chose not to use William James's, because his definition of religious experience as an encounter with "primal reality as the individual feels impelled to respond to solemnly and gravely" unwarrantedly confines religious experience to a particular type of response (James [1902] 1985, 38).

3. For a more exhaustive list of types of religious experiences, see Davis 1989, 29–65.

4. I do not intend to imply by this that one can make a direct and universal correlation between female images in worship and women's religious experiences. I only point out that this was the case for the Bay Chapel and Mount Olive women who were enmeshed in all-female enclaves. Other research suggests a paradoxical rather than causal relationship (Bynum, Harrell, and Richman 1986). It may be that the relationship between sacred female images and female believers' religiosity is influenced by numerous factors, including historical era, features of the specific religious tradition, state of the economy, and so on.

5. As I began interviewing, I discovered that much casual telephoning between congregational women was occurring regarding what possible agenda my research work might have. (I uncovered no evidence of cross-congregational telephoning.) One of my first interviewees reacted in surprise when she realized, midinterview, that I was not questioning her extensively regarding her position on abortion. When I explained that my interest was in women's religious experiences and asked her why she thought it was abortion, she informed me that the woman I interviewed the day before had telephoned and told her that the interview was about abortion. Over time, a sufficient core of women either had questioned me directly about their concerns or been interviewed, or both, that this background noise of fairly misleading gossip about my work died down.

Yet, given the initial levels of distress regarding the tenor of my study, I wondered if some of Elaine's overtly antifeminist comments—especially her statement that "God is male"—were intentional efforts to stretch a distinct gap between her views and what she may have presumed mine to be, as well as between hers and those of any wider audience who might be exposed to my research findings. If so, she was not able to hold the position throughout the study. While Elaine began by declaring herself opposed to feminism, before the interview was over she told me that actually she considered herself a feminist.

6. I am convinced that intriguing insights into significant changes in American culture can be discovered through further research comparing how early American evangelicalism exploited the cultural fear of death to drive people into their folds (Ryan 1981, 88) with the way Bay Chapel, Mount Olive, and their various counterparts in American Christianity now exploit the cultural fear of divorce and family disintegration to accomplish the same ends.

7. This is not to argue that the symbolic world participants encountered at Bay Chapel or Mount Olive was monolithic or that all adherents comprehended it in exactly the same way. Though fundamentalist institutions define the religious truth contained within their worldview in unequivocal terms and therefore are more easy to generalize about than nonfundamentalist institutions (Peshkin 1986, 260), religious

symbols are polysemic (Turner 1967). They have the capacity to exude a variety of meanings, not all necessarily connected to their most obvious one. I explore the possible significance of this for women's religious ideas and experiences in the concluding section of this chapter. What I develop here is a rough map of the symbolic world that authoritative leaders of Mount Olive and Bay Chapel elaborated, followed by a discussion of the paths that believing women were taking through it—always keeping in mind that, as Jonathan Z. Smith cogently argued, "map is not territory" (Smith [1978] 1993). (See chapter 3 regarding the enigmatic role women played in constructing and distributing congregational symbolic capital.)

8. Two important qualifications must be made regarding the innovativeness of Hope Chapel's and Calvary Chapel's music. First, the music that permeates these movements is popular with other religious groups, who also participate in its creation. Second, while it is innovative in the use of rhythm and instrumentation, the theological messages of the songs are not.

9. As biblical scholars disagree on what biblical texts imply about the roles of women in the church, and theologians disagree on the significance such disputed interpretations should be accorded for the role of women in the church today, to address the issue of the role of biblical texts in establishing or legitimating male dominance of leadership within these movements (i.e., the rationale Bay Chapel and Mount Olive male leaders employ to justify excluding women from a preaching pastorate) would require more attention than I can give within the context of my current research agenda. However, I note with considerable irony that the lineage of both movements is traceable to the ministry of a female evangelist, Aimee Semple McPherson.

10. The problem is further exacerbated by the fact that the male pastoral preaching staffs at Bay Chapel and Mount Olive are not only all male but also all white, while the congregations are racially and ethnically diverse.

11. This situation problematized my research into certain aspects of how gender functioned within the congregations. For the believing women of Mount Olive and Bay Chapel, questions that reflected an interest in whether women and men were treated equally were, at best, inappropriately concerned with religion rather than with biblically informed relationship. As Mary explained it, "That's not a focus that we have on our lives here, so to articulate and give our opinion about it, it's kind of like—well, it's not something I think about everyday. I left that stuff behind as I grew up in the Lord."

12. For a different study pursuing this theme, see Burdick's analysis of late twentieth-century Pentecostal and Roman Catholic women's Bible groups in Brazil (1993).

CHAPTER 5   *The Order of God*

1. Statistics are from congregational and pastoral leadership surveys developed and administered by the Lilly-funded USC research team in 1991–1992.

2. Rich theological/cultural insight could be obtained by comparing the expectations of early Calvinists and late twentieth-century fundamentalists like those who attend Bay Chapel and Mount Olive.

3. This dynamic holds consistently across conservative Protestant congregations. See Ammerman [1987] 1988, Bendroth 1993, Hardacre 1993, and Rose 1988 for a cross-section of examples.

4. Marriage between a believer and a nonbeliever is referred to as an "uneven yoke." Such marriages are acknowledged and tolerated within congregational life but are not considered optimal.

5. The Christian Booksellers Association regularly list Charles Swindoll and James Dobson—each of whom specializes in family issues—as two of the best-selling authors they carry (Bineham 1993). Thus, on family issues, Bay Chapel and Mount Olive share the ideas current in the conservative Protestant mainstream.

6. Although female believers often spoke of their faith using the same or similar language as male believers, the implications of certain beliefs were different for women than for men. Thus, I categorize such shared language as androgynous-seeming rather than strictly androgynous.

7. The perception that American women are in an advantaged state compared to women of other countries was widespread among female fundamentalists. To support this contention, they cited personal observations from mission trips they had made and stories they had heard from the mission trips of others. There was no concern that foreign mission activity provided an inherently problematic platform from which to make such an assessment.

8. It is doubtful that these choices were as attributable to free will as believing women described them. With less remunerative job opportunities than men, women have fewer attractive options outside marriage than men and experience a greater drop in economic status once divorced (Okin 1989).

REFERENCES

Ackermann, Robert J. 1985. *Religion as Critique*. Amherst: University of Massachusetts Press.

Adorno, Theodor W. 1994. *The Stars Down to Earth and Other Essays on the Irrational in Culture*. New York: Routledge.

———. [1962] 1989. *Kierkegaard: Construction of the Aesthetic*. Trans. Robert Hullot-Kentor. Minneapolis: University of Minnesota Press.

Aidala, Angela A. 1985. "Social Change, Gender Roles and New Religious Movements." *Sociological Analysis* 46:3–5.

Albanese, Catherine. 1990. *Nature Religion in America: From the Algonkian Indians to the New Age*. Chicago: University of Chicago Press.

Alston, William P. 1991. *Perceiving God: The Epistemology of Religious Experience*. Ithaca: Cornell University Press.

Ammerman, Nancy T. [1987] 1988. *Bible Believers: Fundamentalists in the Modern World*. New Brunswick: Rutgers University Press.

Arthur, Kay. 1991. *Lord, Is It Warfare? Teach Me To Stand*. Portland: Multnomah.

Bainbridge, William Sims. 1992. "The Sociology of Conversion." In *Handbook of Religious Conversion*, ed. H. Newton Malony and Samuel Southard. Birmingham: Religious Education.

Ballmer, Randall. 1992. *Mine Eyes Have Seen the Glory: A Journey into the Evangelical Subculture in America*. New York: Oxford University Press.

Banner, Lois. [1974] 1995. *Women in Modern America: A Brief History*. 3d ed. Fort Worth: Harcourt Brace.

Barr, James. [1977] 1981. *Fundamentalism*. London: SCM.

Batson, C. Daniel, Patricia Schoenrade, and W. Larry Ventis. 1993. *Religion and the Individual: A Social-Psychological Perspective*. 2d ed. New York: Oxford University Press.

Baudrillard, Jean. 1983. *Simulations*. New York: Semiotext(e).

Beaver, R. Pierce. 1968. *All Loves Excelling: American Protestant Women in World Mission*. Grand Rapids: Eerdmans.

Bendroth, Margaret L. 1984. "The Search for 'Women's Role' in American Evangelicalism, 1930–1980" in *Evangelicalism and Modern America*. Grand Rapids: Eerdmans.

———. 1993. *Fundamentalism and Gender: 1875 to the Present*. New Haven: Yale University Press.

Berger, Peter L. 1963. *Invitation to Sociology: A Humanistic Perspective*. New York: Doubleday.

Berger, Peter L., and Thomas Luckmann. 1967. *The Social Construction of Reality: A Treatise in the Sociology of Knowledge*. Garden City: Doubleday.

Bineham, Jeffery L. 1993. "Theological Hegemony and Oppositional Interpretive Codes: The Case of Evangelical Christian Feminism." *Western Journal of Communication* 57,4: 515–529.

Blee, Kathleen M. 1991. *Women of the Klan: Racism and Gender in the 1920s*. Berkeley: University of California Press.

Blumhofer, Edith L. 1993. *Aimee Semple McPherson: Everybody's Sister*. Grand Rapids: Eerdmans.

Boone, Kathleen C. 1989. *The Bible Tells Them So: The Discourse of Protestant Fundamentalism*. New York: State University of New York Press.

Braude, Ann. 1995. "Forum: Female Experience in American Culture." *Religion and American Culture: A Journal of Interpretation* 5, 1: 1–21.

———. 1995. "The Perils of Passivity: Women's—Leadership in Spiritualism and Christian Science." In *Women's Leadership in Marginal Religions: Explorations Outside the Mainstream*, ed. Catherine Wessinger. Urbana: University of Illinois Press.

Brereton, Virginia L. 1991. *From Sin to Salvation: Stories of Women's Conversions, 1800 to the Present*. Bloomington: Indiana University Press.

Brownmiller, Susan. 1984. *Femininity*. New York: Linden/Simon & Schuster.

Burdick, John. 1993. *Looking for God in Brazil: The Progressive Catholic Church in Urban Brazil's Religious Arena*. Berkeley: University of California Press.

Butler, Jon. 1990. *Awash in a Sea of Faith: Christianizing the American People*. Cambridge: Harvard University Press.

Cott, Nancy F. 1977. *The Bonds of Womanhood: Woman's Sphere in New England 1780–1835*. New Haven: Yale University Press.

Daly, Mary. 1968. *The Church and the Second Sex*. New York: Harper & Row.

Davidman, Lynn. 1991. *Tradition in a Rootless World: Women Turn to Orthodox Judaism*. Berkeley: University of California Press.

Davis, Caroline Franks. 1989. *The Evidential Force of Religious Experience*. Oxford: Clarendon.

DeBerg, Betty A. 1990. *Ungodly Women: Gender and the First Wave of American Fundamentalism*. Minneapolis: Fortress.

Diamond, Sara. 1989. *Spiritual Warfare: The Politics of the New Christian Right*. Boston: South End.

Dinnerstein, Dorothy. 1976. *The Mermaid and The Minotaur: Sexual Arrangements and Human Malaise*. New York: Harper & Row.

Douglas, Ann. 1977. *The Feminization of American Culture*. New York: Knopf.

Dworkin, Andrea. 1983. *Right-Wing Women*. New York: Wideview/Perigee.

Eisenstein, Zillah R. 1982. "The Sexual Politics of the New Right: Understanding the 'Crisis of Liberalism' for the 1980s." *Signs: Journal of Women in Culture and Society* 7, 3: 567–588.

Eliade, Mircea. 1959. *The Sacred and the Profane: The Nature of Religion*. New York: Harcourt Brace Jovanovich.

Ellwood, Robert S. 1973. *One Way: The Jesus Movement and Its Meaning*. Englewood Cliffs: Prentice-Hall.

Enroth, Ronald M., Edward E. Ericson, Jr., and C. Breckinridge Peters. 1972. *The Jesus People: Old Time Religion in the Age of Aquarius*. Grand Rapids: Eerdmanns.

Epstein, Cynthia Fuchs. 1988. *Deceptive Distinctions: Sex, Gender and the Social Order*. New Haven: Yale University Press.

Epstein, Daniel Mark. 1993. *Sister Aimee: The Life of Aimee Semple McPherson*. New York: Harcourt Brace Jovanovich.

Erickson, Victoria Lee. 1993. *Where Silence Speaks: Feminism, Social Theory and Religion*. Minneapolis: Fortress.

Falwell, Jerry. 1981. *The Fundamentalist Phenomenon*. Garden City: Doubleday.

Fitzgerald, Frances, [1981] 1986. *Cities on a Hill: A Journey through Contemporary American Cultures*. New York: Simon & Schuster.

Frieze Hanson, Irene, and Maureen McHugh. 1992. "Power and Influence Strategies in Violent and Nonviolent Marriages." *Psychology of Women Quarterly* 16, 4: 449–466.

Gillespie, Joanna Bowen. 1995. *Women Speak: Of God, Congregations and Change*. Valley Forge: Trinity Press International.

Goldenberg, Naomi R. 1979. *Changing of the Gods: Feminism and the End of Traditional Religions*. Boston: Beacon.

Gordon, David F. 1984. "Dying to Self: Self-Control through Self-Abandonment." *Sociological Analysis* 45, 1: 45–56.

Greig, Doris. 1985. "Study in the Book of Acts." In *Joy of Living Bible Studies*. Oak View, Calif.: Joy of Living Bible Studies.

Hadden, Jeffrey K., and Anson Shupe. 1988. *Televangelism: Power and Politics on God's Frontier*. New York: Henry Holt.

Hagestad, Grunhild O. 1984. "Women in Intergenerational Patterns of Power and Influence." In *Social Power and Influence of Women*, ed. Liesa Stamm and Carol D. Ryff. Boulder: Westview.

Handy, Robert. 1984. *A Christian America: Protestant Hopes and Historical Realities*. New York: Oxford University Press.

Hardacre, Helen. 1993. "The Impact of Fundamentalisms on Women, the Family, and Interpersonal Relations." In *Fundamentalisms and Society*, ed. Martin E. Marty and R. Scott Appleby. Chicago: University of Chicago Press.

Harder, Mary White, James T. Richardson, and Robert B. Simmonds. 1972. "Jesus People." *Psychology Today*, December, 45–49.

Hatch, Nathan O. 1989. *The Democratization of American Christianity*. New Haven: Yale University Press.

Hawley, John Stratton, ed. 1993. *Fundamentalism and Gender*. New York: Oxford University Press.

Higginbotham, Evelyn. 1993. *Righteous Discontent: The Women's Movement in the Black Baptist Church: 1800–1920*. Cambridge: Harvard University Press.

Himmelstein, Jerome L. 1986. "The Social Basis of Antifeminism: Religious Networks and Culture." *Journal for the Scientific Study of Religion* 25, 1: 63–74.

Holte, James Craig. 1992. *The Conversion Experience in America: A Sourcebook on Religious Conversion Autobiography*. New York: Greenwood.

Hunter, James Davison. 1983. *American Evangelicalism: Conservative Religion and the Quandary of Modernity*. New Brunswick: Rutgers University Press.

————. 1987. *Evangelicalism: The Coming Generation*. Chicago: University of Chicago Press.

Iannaccone, Laurence. 1995. "Rational Choice: Framework for the Scientific Study of Religion." In *Rational Choice Theory and Religion: Summary and Assessment*, ed. Larry Young. New York: Routledge.

————. 1995. "Voodoo Economics? Reviewing the Rational Choice Approach to Religion." *Journal for the Scientific Study of Religion* 34, 1: 76–88.

Iannaccone, Laurence, and Carrie Miles. 1990. "Dealing with Social Change: The Mormon Church's Response to Change in Women's Roles." *Social Forces* 68, 4: 1231–1250.

James, Janet Wilson, ed. [1980] 1989. *Women in American Religion*. Philadelphia: University of Pennsylvania Press.

James, William. [1902] 1985. *The Varieties of Religious Experience: A Study in Human Nature*. New York: Penguin.

Jung, Carl Gustav. 1938. *Psychology and Religion*. New Haven: Yale University Press.

Kandiyoti, Deniz. 1988. "Bargaining with Patriarchy." Gender and Society 2 (September): 274–290.

Kirkpatrick, Lee A. 1993. "Fundamentalism, Christian Orthodoxy and Intrinsic Religious Orientation as Predictors of Discriminatory Attitudes." *Journal for the Scientific Study of Religion* 32, 3: 256–268.

Klatch, Rebecca E. 1987. *Women of the New Right*. Philadelphia: Temple University Press.

Kosmin, Barry A., and Seymour P. Lachman. 1993. *One Nation under God: Religion in Contemporary American Society*. New York: Harmony.

Lawrence, Bruce B. 1989. *Defenders of God: The Fundamentalist Revolt against the Modern Age*. San Francisco: Harper & Row.

Leghorn, Lisa, and Katherine Parker. 1981. *Woman's Worth: Sexual Economics in the World of Women*. Boston: Routledge & Kegan Paul.

Lengermann, Patricia Madoo, and Ruth A. Wallace. 1985. *Gender in America: Social Control and Social Change*. Englewood Cliffs: Prentice-Hall.

Lerner, Gerda. 1986. *The Creation of Patriarchy*. New York: Oxford University Press.

————. 1993. *The Creation of Feminist Consciousness: From the Middle Ages to Eighteen-Seventy*. New York: Oxford University Press.

Lofland, John, and Peter Stark. 1965. "Becoming a World-Saver: A Theory of Conversion to a Deviant Perspective." *American Sociological Review* 30:862–875.

Luker, Kristen. 1984. *Abortion and the Politics of Motherhood*. Berkeley: University of California Press.

Lyotard, Jean-François, and Jean-Loup Thébaud. 1985. *Just Gaming*. Minneapolis: University of Minnesota Press.

MacIntosh, Michael, and Raul Ries. 1992. *A Venture in Faith: The History and Philosophy of the Calvary Chapel Movement*. Diamond Bar, Calif.: Logos Media Group. Videotape.

McNamara, Patrick. 1985. "Conservative Christian Families and Their Moral World: Some Reflections for Sociologists." *Sociological Analysis* 46, 2: 98–105.

Marsden, George M. [1980] 1982. *Fundamentalism and American Culture: The Shaping of Twentieth-Century Evangelicalism 1870–1925*. Oxford: Oxford University Press.

————. 1991. *Understanding Fundamentalism and Evangelicalism*. Grand Rapids: Eerdmans.

Marty, Martin E., and R. Scott Appleby, eds. 1991. *Fundamentalisms Observed*. Chicago: University of Chicago Press.

————. 1992. *The Glory and the Power: The Fundamentalist Challenge to the Modern World*. Boston: Beacon.

Miller, Timothy, ed. 1991. *When Prophets Die: The Postcharismatic Fate of New Religious Movements*. New York: State University of New York Press.

Neitz, Mary Jo. 1987. *Charisma and Community: A Study of Religious Commitment within the Charismatic Renewal*. New Brunswick: Transaction.

————. 1993. *A Future for Religion? New Paradigms for Social Analysis*. Newbury Park, Conn.: Sage.

Neuhaus, Richard John, and Michael Cromartie. 1987. *Piety and Politics: Evangelicals and Fundamentalists Confront the World*. Washington: Ethics and Public Policy Center.

Neville, Gwen Kennedy. 1974. "Religious Socialization of Women within U.S. Subcultures." In *Sexist Religion and Women in the Church: No More Silence!* ed. Alice L. Hageman. New York: Association.

O'Leary, Stephen D. 1994. *Arguing the Apocalypse: A Theory of Millennial Rhetoric*. New York: Oxford University Press.

Okin, Susan Moller. 1989. *Justice, Gender, and the Family*. New York: Basic.

Otto, Rudolf. [1923] 1950. *The Idea of the Holy*. New York: Oxford University Press.

Padilla, Angela Lucia. 1987. *Subordinant but Not Inferior: Women in the New Christian Right*. B.A. thesis, Harvard and Radcliffe Colleges.

Palmer, Susan J. 1993. "Women's 'Cocoon Work' in New Religious Movements: Sexual Experimentation and Feminine Rites of Passage." *Journal for the Scientific Study of Religion* 32, 4: 343–355.

———. 1994. *Moon Sisters, Krishna Mothers, Rajneesh Lovers: Women's Roles in New Religions*. Syracuse: Syracuse University Press.

Perrin, Robin D., and Armand L. Mauss. 1993. "Strictly Speaking . . . : Kelley's Quandary and the Vineyard Christian Fellowship." *Journal for the Scientific Study of Religion* 32, 2: 125–135.

Plaskow, Judith. [1990] 1991. *Standing Again at Sinai: Judaism from a Feminist Perspective*. San Francisco: HarperCollins.

Proudfoot, Wayne. 1976. *God and the Self: Three Types of Philosophy of Religion*. Lewisburg: Bucknell University Press.

Radl, Shirley Rogers. 1983. *The Invisible Woman: Target of the New Religious Right*. New York: Delacorte.

Rambo, Lewis R. 1993. *Understanding Religious Conversion*. New Haven: Yale University Press.

Rando, Therese A., ed. 1986. *Parental Loss of a Child*. Champaign, Ill.: Research.

Rapp, Rayna. 1988. "Is the Legacy of Second Wave Feminism Postfeminism?" *Socialist Review* 97 (June): 31–37.

Rhode, Deborah L. 1995. "Media Images, Feminist Issues." *Signs: Journal of Women in Culture and Society* 20, 3: 685–710.

Richardson, James T., and Rex Davis. 1983. "Experiential Fundamentalism: Revisions of Orthodoxy in the Jesus Movement." *Journal of the American Academy of Religion* 51, 3: 397–425.

Rieserbrodt, Martin. [1990] 1993. *Pious Passion: The Emergence of Modern Fundamentalism in the United States and Iran*. Berkeley: University of California Press.

Rogers, Susan C. 1975. "Female Forms of Power and the Myth of Male Dominance: A Model of Female/Male Interaction in Peasant Society." *American Ethnologist* 2: 125–129.

Roof, Wade Clark. 1993. *A Generation of Seekers: The Spiritual Journey of the Baby Boom Generation*. San Francisco: HarperSanFrancisco.

Roof, Wade Clark, and William McKinney. 1987. *American Mainline Religion: Its Changing Shape and Future*. New Brunswick: Rutgers University Press.

Rosaldo, Michelle L. 1974. *Women, Culture and Society: A Theoretical Overview*. Stanford: Stanford University Press.

Rose, Susan D. 1987. "Women Warriors: The Negotiation of Gender Roles in an Evangelical Community." *Sociological Analysis* 48, 3: 245–258.

————. 1988. *Keeping Them Out of the Hands of Satan: Evangelical Schooling in America*. New York: Routledge, Chapman and Hall.

Rosenfelt, Deborah, and Judith Stacey. 1987. "Second Thoughts on the Second Wave." *Feminist Studies* 13, 2: 341–361.

Ruether, Rosemary Radford, and Rosemary Skinner Keller, eds. 1986. *Women and Religion in America*. Volume 3, *1900–1968*. San Francisco: Harper & Row.

Ryan, Mary P. 1981. *Cradle of the Middle Class: The Family in Oneida County, New York, 1790–1865*. New York: Cambridge University Press.

Sanday, Peggy Reeves. 1981. *Female Power and Male Dominance: On the Origins of Sexual Inequality*. New York: Cambridge University Press.

Schussler-Fiorenza, Elisabeth. 1990. *In Memory of Her: A Feminist Theological Reconstruction of Christian Origins*. New York: Crossroads.

Segal, Lynne. 1987. *Is the Future Female? Troubled Thoughts on Contemporary Feminism*. New York: Peter Bedrick.

Simpson, John H. 1992. "Fundamentalism in America Revisited." In *Religion and Politics in Comparative Perspective*, ed. B. Misztal and A. Shupe. Westport, Conn.: Praeger.

Smith, Dorothy E. 1990. *The Conceptual Practices of Power: A Feminist Sociology of Knowledge*. Boston: Northeastern University Press.

Smith, Jonathan Z. [1978] 1993. *Map Is Not Territory*. Chicago: University of Chicago Press.

Sorenson, Ann Marie, Carl F. Grindstaff, and R. Jay Turner. 1995. "Religious Involvement among Unmarried Adolescent Mothers: A Source of Emotional Support?" *Sociology of Religion* 56, 1: 71–81.

Stacey, Judith. 1990. *Brave New Families: Stories of Domestic Upheaval in Late Twentieth Century America*. New York: Basic.

Staples, Clifford, and Armand L. Mauss. 1987. "Conversion or Commitment? A Reassessment of the Snow and Machalek Approach." *Journal for the Scientific Study of Religion* 26, 2: 133–147.

Stark, Rodney. 1965. "A Taxonomy of Religious Experience." *Journal for the Scientific Study of Religion* 4, 5: 97–116.

Stark, Rodney, and William Sims Bainbridge. 1985. *The Future of Religion: Secularization, Revival and Cult Formation*. Berkeley: University of California Press.

Stein, Gertrude. 1928. *Useful Knowledge*. New York: Payson & Clarke.

Straus, Murray, and Richard Gelles. 1990. *Physical Violence in American Families*. New Brunswick: Transaction.

Swatos Jr., William H., ed. 1993. *Gender and Religion*. New Brunswick: Transaction.

Tillich, Paul. 1967. *A History of Christian Thought: From Its Judaic and Hellenistic Origins to Existentialism*. Ed. Carl E. Braaten. New York: Simon & Schuster.

Tilly, Louise A., and Patricia Gurin, eds. 1990. *Women, Politics and Change*. New York: Russell Sage.

Troeltsch, Ernst. [1911] 1981. *The Social Teachings of the Christian*

Churches. Vol. 2. Trans. Olive Wyon. Chicago: Chicago University Press.

Wagner, Melina Bollar. 1990. *God's Schools: Choice and Compromise in American Society*. New Brunswick: Rutgers University Press.

Wallace, Ruth. 1992. *They Call Her Pastor: A New Role for Catholic Women*. Albany: State University of New York Press.

Warner, R. Stephen. 1993. "Work in Progress toward a New Paradigm for the Sociological Study of Religion in the United States." *American Journal of Sociology* 98, 5: 1044–1092.

Weber, Max. [1922] 1963. *The Sociology of Religion*. Boston: Beacon.

———. [1947] 1964. *The Theory of Social and Economic Organization*. New York: Free.

Willard, Ann. 1988. "Cultural Scripts for Mothering." In *Mapping the Moral Domain*. Cambridge: Harvard University Press.

Wind, James P., and James W. Lewis, eds. 1994. *American Congregations*. Chicago: University of Chicago Press.

Wuthnow, Robert. 1987. *The Restructuring of American Religion*. Princeton: Princeton University Press.

Young, Iris Marion. 1990. *Throwing like a Girl and Other Essays in Feminist Philosophy and Social Theory*. Bloomington: Indiana University Press.

Zikmund, Barbara Brown. 1986. "Winning Ordination for Women in Mainstream Protestant Churches." In *Women and Religion in America*, ed. Rosemary Radford Ruether and Rosemary Skinner Keller. Vol. 3, *1900–1968*. San Francisco: Harper & Row.

INDEX

About the Author

Brenda E. Brasher, an assistant professor of religion and philosophy at Mount Union College, received her master's degree in divinity from Christian Theological Seminary and completed her doctorate in religion (social ethics) at the University of Southern California. She has published articles in a variety of scholarly journals. Her next project is a study of religion and cyberspace.